THE

FIELD GUIDE TO NORTH AMERICAN MALES

Marjorie Ingall

AN OWL BOOK

HENRY HOLT AND COMPANY

NEW YORK

Henry Holt and Company, Inc.
Publishers since 1866
115 West 18th Street
New York, New York 10011

Henry Holt® is a registered
trademark of Henry Holt and Company, Inc.

Library of Congress Cataloging-in-Publication Data
Ingall, Marjorie.
The field guide to North American males /
Marjorie Ingall. — 1st ed.
p.   cm.
"An Owl book."
ISBN 0-8050-4219-9
1. Men—North America—Humor.   I. Title.
PN6231.M45I54   1996   96-27509
818'.5407—dc20   CIP

Henry Holt books are available for special
promotions and premiums. For details contact:
Director, Special Markets.

First Edition—1997

Designed by Victoria Hartman

Printed in the United States of America
All first editions are printed on acid-free paper. ∞

1   3   5   7   9   10   8   6   4   2

Acknowledgments

◈

Appreciation is due to the following males, who allowed themselves to be netted, cleaned of oil, tagged, and examined: Aaron Foeste *(Vanbiesbrouck lindros)*, Justin Hall *(Notatus caeruleus)*, Dale Hrabi *(Overdere eh)*, Andy Ingall *(Stellaus stellaus)*, and Rick Schneider *(Birdona wire)*.

Further assistance was provided by my brilliant female associates—Cynthia Cohen, Danielle Claro, Mara, MP Dunleavey, Lynn Harris, Allison Jernow, Carol Ingall, and Heather Weston; as well as my wise editors, Jennifer Unter and Tracy Sherrod; and my agent, Gordon Kato. Extra thanks go to Ellen Forney, the most gifted and patient scientific illustrator in the land.

And finally, head-bobs to Jonathan Steuer, alpha male of all *Cyberdorkus perpetui*.

Contents

◈

Introduction

◇

WHY A FIELD GUIDE?

Human males can be so baffling: a vast, undifferentiated hairy mass of beings, darting around the periphery of your vision like common wrens. Wouldn't it be lovely if the world of men were just as neatly classifiable as that of the animal kingdom? If there were some means of imposing order on the unruly, random boy universe?

The *The Field Guide to North American Males* is the answer. Like a handy bird guide, *The Field Guide to North American Males* breaks down the often puzzling male population into discrete species for easier categorization. Suddenly, the mythological, potent male animal is something far less intimidating, cuter and more understandable—much like a little sparrow.

Bird guides let the baffled birder feel in control. The user quickly learns to recognize and name certain species. What a delicious feeling of mastery this bestows! Yet until now, there has never been a similar classification for human males. Where can they be found? What do they eat? What are their courtship and mating behaviors? Understanding that men fall into separate species, with differing traits and biological imperatives, is the key to recognizing their foibles and pitfalls. This keeps the clever female from becoming prey.

When a female without *The Field Guide to North American Males* is confronted with a mysterious, stubbly member of the male family, she may not know how to react. But with the field guide in hand, she can quickly consult the appropriate family (Artsy, Gainfully Employed, Athletic, or Casual), use the description of plumage to find the exact species or subspecies within that genus, and handle said male accordingly. For example, a female who knows the quirks of a particular species won't waste time, money, and energy feeding a Painfully Sincere Activist Guy (*Boycottus grapesus*) baby veal with mango chutney instead of a soyburger. Knowledge is power.

I modestly acknowledge my role as the new Darwin, setting sail on the HMS *Beagle* on a quest that will benefit single women for years to come. But unlike the big snooze that is *The Origin of Species*, *The Field Guide to North American Males* is visually interesting, interactive, and fun. After all, boy-watching is an entertaining activity—and a novel one. For years, women were supposed to be on display but never to look back. Today, women can leer and dissect and analyze as much as boys can, but they still need a little coaching, a little guidance, a little direction to the appraising stare (unlike men, who as we all know need no prodding). Therefore, the *Field Guide*'s tone is reassuring (you can develop your skills!) as well as inspiring (get out there! you'll learn something!) while offering enough common-sense warnings (certain species are dangerous, and here's how to tell which ones) to prepare the emerging naturalist.

HOW TO USE THIS BOOK

Every year more than half a million birds are scooped up in nets and tagged by the U.S. Fish and Wildlife Service. This helps us understand migration patterns and site fidelity to breeding areas. It would be great if we could similarly take a confirmed sleazy male and put a tag around his leg so other women would see it and know to avoid him. Unfortunately, this is illegal. Likewise, it would be great to use Doppler radar to measure how quickly a given male runs away when you threaten him with a commitment, or how quickly he runs toward a recording deal or a Twinkie or a fashion model. Unfortunately, this is impossible. The only recourse females have is to read this book, learn to distinguish the different species and their foibles, and *share the information* with other women.

Bring this small volume into the field. If you spot an interesting male engaged in grooming or foraging behavior, take notes. How does he tie his shoe, flirt with a passing waitress, eat a bagel? Be as unobtrusive as possible—you are an observer, not a participant. Do not steal eggs from nests, riffle through briefcases, or feed the male.

Be alert to opportunities to contribute to the body of existing male-watching data, adding to the domain of knowledge by donating your field notes, after your death, to any of several cooperative research projects (write to Marjorie Ingall, *The Field Guide to North American Males*, c/o Henry Holt and

Company, 115 West 18th Street, New York, NY 10011 for a list). You might also publish your findings in any of a number of local, regional, and national scientific journals, such as *YM* and *Cosmo*. Please check our web site, at www.fieldguide.com, for updated information as well as ways you can aid us in this vital quest.

As yet, no reputable university offers a degree program in male-watching. *The Field Guide to North American Males* team is entirely self-trained. We are not professional ethologists (researchers of animal behavior), anthropologists, ornithologists, or social scientists. How did we gain this specialized knowledge? By dating many, many boys. According to our own calculations, we've dated 34 of the 57 species herein. (By "we," we of course mean "I," in the universally recognized lofty scientific manner of expression.)

Remember, the scope of males available to you is as broad as the entire range of male humanity: distinguished older gentlemen, "boy toys," creative types, exotic men of different nationalities, various professionals, and blue-collar workers. No matter what your "type" is, you'll find him in the guide. Please make full use of the extensive illustrations, memorizing each species' characteristics and noting its distinctive markings, so that when you're out in the field, you won't have to keep thumbing through the book (possibly missing a given specimen as he darts by). The appendices will add to your knowledge, offering advice on the foibles of particular species and hints about whether they are good prospects for mating. After all, you deserve the best genetic material! You're worth it!

Why You Should Consider Looking Without Disturbing the Natural Habitat

Alas, women are relentlessly bombarded with messages saying we are nothing without a man. This book argues that while having a boyfriend is appealing, one should not become delusional. You could choose just to watch instead of dating constantly. You should never stay with an unsuitable male just because you "need" to have a boyfriend. Why can't you just have a good time for a while? Why try to domesticate any given species? Ignore the societal messages telling you to put out nets, snare your wildlife, and drag it home. This is environmentally unfriendly!

Some Important Terms

LEKS: A lek, to zoologists, is a breeding area where males of a species gather to strut and preen. During estrus (horniness times), females show up to check out the available talent. Human male leks include pool halls, jazz clubs, batting cages, hardware stores, computer stores, sound and lighting boards of community theaters, and the Internet. When you're in estrus, go for it.

SEXUAL SELECTION: This principle states that the males who get the best spots on a lek (the dominant males) get more chances to mate with females. (It really is true that having lots of money, a cool apartment, and the power booth at a restaurant conveys certain advantages.) But remember that in lekking species, females do not stay with males after mating. In other words, you will not meet your mate for life at a singles bar. Look beyond the instant signifiers of dominance into the soul of the male in question. That's where you will discover if he is worth pair-bonding with.

SITE FIDELITY: This is when birds return to the same nesting or breeding sites over and over. Human males may show site fidelity to specific bars, basketball courts, movies starring specific actors, particular paintings in museums. The male associates these settings with prior reproductive success, or at the very least, a sense of familiarity and safety.

ALPHA MALE: The alpha male is the most dominant member of a flock or herd. The other animals copy his behavior and treat him deferentially. Among Gangly Foxy Basketball Players, the alpha male is Michael Jordan. Among High-Strung Chefs, it is James Beard. Among Happy Musical Theater Fellas, it is Gene Kelly.

UNDERSTANDING THE LISTINGS

Our 57 North American Male descriptions start with the given male's vernacular or **common name,** and then tell you his **scientific name.** The scientific name consists of two Latin, Greek, or completely invented words. The first word, always capitalized, indicates the genus to which the male belongs. The second refers to the species within the genus. For this wonderful system, we may thank the anal-retentive Swedish naturalist Linnaeus, who had a compulsive need to name all the plants and animals on the planet. Because he lived in the eighteenth century, he did not receive the psychiatric help he so clearly needed.

Each listing then moves on to discuss the **diet, nest type, financial intake,** and **foraging technique** of the male in question. Each of these items is represented by an adorable icon. A key to the icons is on page 8.

The listing goes on to discuss **plumage** (identifying physical features, listed in order of prominence to facilitate quick identification), **habitat** (where the species lives, what its nest contains, what areas it frequents), and **feeding habits** (what it eats, and where).

From there it goes on to displays. Displays are the way a bird or human male uses his body to convey information. When he puffs his chest and performs particular vocalizations, he is letting females and other males know something important about himself. The act of grooming and strutting in certain ways as an attempt to impress and pick up females is called a **sexual display.** The act of taking an agonistic, or aggressive, posture against subordinate birds and males because the individual feels threatened or angered is called an **agonistic display.**

Then the listing details **courtship behavior** (what the male does while wooing the female, or "what you do on a date," to use the lay expression), **mating rituals** (what the male habitually does as a prelude to, during, and/or immediately after sexual intercourse), **mating call** (how the male vocally makes his desires known), and **field notes** (any additional information that might be of use to the interested ethologist).

This book is meant to serve as your companion in the field. We hope you find it useful. May the male-watching be colorful wherever you go!

KEY TO SYMBOLS

Diet

Takeout Chinese =

Health food =

Meat 'n' potatoes =

Protein shake =

Seared salmon =

Twinkies =

Other =

Nest type

Dumpster =

Foreign land =

Mother's house =

Penthouse =

Tent =

Tenement =

Tract house =

Other/varies =

Intake

Dirt poor =

Makes a living =

Makes a nice living =

Stinking rich =

uncertain =

Foraging techniques

(In ornithology, this refers to how birds get food. In human ethology, it refers to how males approach females.)

foliage glean = male hangs out in the same territory as female, gradually striking up conversation about the setting or common interest

ground glean = male is shy, doesn't make much eye contact

hover and pounce = male pursues female very aggressively

probes = male's approach is thoughtful, questioning

stalk and strike = male is scary

surface dives = male's passes are shallow, casual

THE

NORTH
AMERICAN
MALES

Family: Artsy

Pretentious Serious Theater Man	*Stellaus stellaus*
Happy Musical Theater Fella	*Rogers anhammerstein*
Baffling Performance Artist	*ArtsGrantus nono*
Alienated Film Boy	*Royalus withcheesum*
Heavy-Lidded Jazz Aficionado	*Notatus caeruleus*
Smooth 'n' Oily Lounge Act	*Igottabeme crooner*
Hathead Country-Western Singer	*Yodelus heehaw*
Snarling Gangsta Rapper	*Lass lassie pooch*
Pissy Pierced Punk	*AAAAAARGH eeeeeauhhhcccchh huh huh huh*
Alternative Rock Boy	*Cobainus howlum*
Acerbic Bipolar Novelist	*Burroughs kerouacum*
Starving Disaffected Art Male	*Piccasus basquiatum*

About Artistic Boys

The tortured, artistic young man is always appealing. Our salivatory response to him has been imprinted upon us by exposure to countless foxy historical and cultural role models: William Butler Yeats, Vincent van Gogh, Arthur Rimbaud, Johnny Depp, Jean-Michel Basquiat, Joseph (biblical), Franz Liszt, Jim Morrison, Brick in *Cat on a Hot Tin Roof,* River Phoenix, Dracula, Jesus, and all famous people named Dylan.

Why is the artsy male so often more enticing than the Gainfully Employed male? Because of his big emotions and flaming passions; his intensity; his hooded, drawn, Daniel Day-Lewis–like countenance; his ego and his glamor. He is not boring. Yet that is precisely why a relationship with him is so difficult. The artsy male can be very manipulative. He is unreliable; he is unlikely ever to value a mortal female above his Art. Yet social intercourse with the artsy male can be fulfilling if the female learns to appreciate his inherent cuteness and torment while maintaining her independence and refraining from too much investment in his pain.

Pretentious Serious Theater Man
(*Stellaus stellaus*)

Diet:

Nest Type:

Intake:

Foraging Technique:

Plumage: Plumage is unfailingly black. If the observed male is wearing bright, uplifting color, he is probably the Happy Musical Theater Fella. Cigarette (regular or clove) dangles from lips or fingertips. Kiehl's hair products, used to simulate greasy hair, or actual unwashed hair grease. Stubble. Sneer. Dark jeans hang from his narrow hips. Clunky, comfortable shoes facilitate running from unsuccessful audition to unsuccessful audition.

Habitat: Wee alternative community theater. Video store, renting *Throne of Blood* or *Raging Bull*. Theatrical bookstore, reading Albee, Artaud, Bataille, Beckett, Brecht, Foreman, Ionesco, Mamet, O'Neill, Sartre, Schechner, Shepard, Stoppard, Shakespeare, or any new work that involves non sequiturs, nudity, and screaming. On subway, staring alternately at photocopied, highlighted page of audition monologue and at the ceiling while

gesticulating and moving lips. (Note: Do not confuse the Pretentious Serious Theater Man with the Delusional Schizophrenic, who does the same thing without the photocopied piece of paper.) Neighborhood bistro, sullenly reciting specials and sighing heavily.

Feeding Habits: Caviar taste, Kit-Kat budget. The *Stellaus stellaus* is knowledgeable about fine food and wine, and frequently works as a waiter or catering slave while plying his craft, yet he cannot himself afford to eat the way he feels he deserves to eat. This is his burden. He chooses whole-grain cereals and items low in fat; he needs to keep his edge. Spot him buying fresh fruits and vegetables at the stand on the street near the theater. Watch as he turns the nutritive experience into an acting challenge, telling himself to visibly savor the peach or seductively eat the banana.

Sexual Display: The authoritative voice—strong and clear or low and seductive, projected from the diaphragm. If you encounter the Pretentious Serious Theater Man at a party, he will place your hand firmly on his diaphragm to show you how he Projects. This may or may not be a courtship ritual—he is so self-absorbed, he may be unaware that touching his body might be construed as an intimate act. Expect calculated eye-crinkling smiles, faux-hearty laughter, seemingly spellbound eye contact. Talking incessantly about himself is his modus operandi. All day, every day. He may or may not be hitting on you.

Agonistic Display: No fisticuffs—his face is his fortune. Unless, of course, he is of the Sean Penn school, believing that a thrice-broken nose lends character and a reputation for violence enhances credibility as a Bad Boy of the Theater. Topics sure to foster agonistic behavior include but are not limited to: "You Mean You're a Waiter, Ha Ha," "Why Americans Can't Do Shakespeare," "Method Acting Is a Crock," and "If You Haven't Had Your Big Break Yet Maybe It's Time to Hang It Up and Get a Real Job."

Courtship Behavior: Keeps you on his right side to show off his better profile. Takes you to plays his friends are in. Takes you to vintage film festivals (you pay). Asks you to listen to his audition monologue.

Mating Ritual: Reenacts scenes from *9½ Weeks, Tampopo,* and *Wild Orchid,* acting as if the food games, mild bondage, and sex in rainy subway stations are his own personal, very original idea.

Mating Call: "I want you. But what's my motivation?"

Field Notes: If you are actually interested in a relationship with this species, think Jeanne Moreau in *Jules and Jim.* She acted wild and unpredictable, kept both men who wanted her at arm's length, played them against each other, remained ultimately unknowable, looked wonderful in cropped hair, capris, and striped sailor shirts, and self-destructed in a very glamorous and fatal way. The boys were more obsessed with the idea of her than the reality of her. Fortunately, when a woman is crazy or dead, she makes very few demands that might distract one from one's torment and art.

Happy Musical Theater Fella
(*Rogers anhammerstein*)

Diet: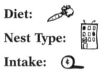

Nest Type:

Intake:

Foraging Technique:

Plumage: Dance gear—tights, legwarmers, loose T-shirt. When not dancing or auditioning, dresses like the well-adjusted, nontormented young man he is: jeans, turtlenecks, T-shirts, clean, new flannel shirts, clean white sneakers. May wear a baseball cap (particularly if he is balding and still going out for juvenile male leads).

Habitat: Waiting on line at the reduced-price ticket booth. Funk aerobics class. Milling around outside the stage door, hoping someone will ask him for an autograph. Video store, renting *West Side Story* or *A Chorus Line*. Theatrical bookstore, looking at posters for *Oklahoma!*, *Guys and Dolls*, *Company*, *Sunday in the Park with George*, *South Pacific*, *Coco*, and *Tommy*. Neighborhood bistro, perkily reciting specials and saying "Good choice!" to every customer no matter what they order.

Feeding Habits: Like the *Stellaus stellaus*, the *Rogers anhammerstein* often works in the food

industry while waiting for his big break. He eats even more healthily than his counterpart in the serious theater (All-Bran, organic produce, Entenmann's fat-free strudel) and displays more neuroses about his body than your average supermodel or ballerina. Watch for evidence of bulimia—a shopping cart loaded with soft, easily regurgitable items like ice cream, overprocessed white bread, and peanut butter is a dead giveaway.

Sexual Display: No mind games, like the ones his brother in the serious theater plays. He is more likely to chirp, "I think you're cute! Do you want to have a drink sometime?" than smolder at you. You may mistake his natural exuberance and curiosity for romantic interest; to avoid embarrassment, be very clear you are reading signals correctly before you spontaneously fasten yourself to his lips. Odds are good that in actuality he prefers the company of other Fellas. While this may take him out of the running as a sexual partner, it makes boy-watching at a café with him that much more fun.

Agonistic Display: Spits out bitchy comments about his rivals' clothes, hair, or complexion.

Courtship Behavior: Invites you to class to watch him dance or do his big scene in Voice & Movement class. Invites you to "his" restaurant, where he winkingly sneaks you extra glasses of wine. Spontaneously breaks into big scene from *Fame* and dances on roofs of cars and edges of fountains.

Mating Ritual: Sings "Where Is Love" from *Oliver!*.

Mating Call: "You know, you look like Audrey Hepburn in *Funny Face*." (Most men do not "get" Audrey Hepburn. The Happy Musical Theater Fella may be the one man you date who appreciates her beauty as much as you do.)

Baffling Performance Artist
(*ArtsGrantus nono*)

Diet:

Nest Type:

Intake:

Foraging Technique:

Plumage: Clad entirely in black (think Dieter on *Sprockets*); or in a kilt, leather chaps, and black ski parka; or in a pink plastic slicker and glittering eyeshadow. Either an utter absence of color or an explosion of vivid plumage. Generally enveloped in a haze of cigarette smoke. May wear clothing made of such unorthodox substances as paper, rubber, film, packing tape, and dried lentils.

Habitat: Never spotted before noon (hibernates). Generally seen in tiny black-box theaters, nightclubs too cool to have names, Weimar-feeling cabarets, drag shows, piercing emporiums. Attracted to velvet surfaces, on which he lounges like a cat, always smoking, smoking. His black- or red-walled home is filled with billowing curtains and bare walls, with the bed invariably placed at a diagonal in the middle of the floor.

Feeding Habits: Eats when he remembers, obsessed as he is with his Art at all times. Unfortunately, prone to drinking or injecting his dinner. Enjoys mooching off the "bourgeois pigs" whenever possible (definition: anyone with a steady job). Not averse to crashing bar mitzvahs, weddings, and funerals while wearing a silver bodysuit, for laughs and munchies.

Sexual Display: Nails naked self to living-room floor, then invites people over. Presents women with pinecones and bits of string.

Agonistic Display: Talks loudly about his heroin habit with your parents or employer.

Courtship Behavior: Takes you to performances of fellow *ArtsGrantus nonos.* Evenings of watching body painting, viewing walls of monitors showing static, listening to Yoko Ono records, and watching Andy Warhol films of people sitting in chairs and smoking cigarettes for four hours.

Mating Ritual: Paints your name in his own blood on his torso.

Mating Call: "Please wear my nipple ring."

Field Notes: When intimidated by members of the Performance Art pack, remember that you need but a two-word vocabulary. In either case, keep your face entirely blank as you watch the art. Then shut your eyes, part your lips slightly and breathe one of the following two words: "Revelatory" or "Derivative." If asked to elaborate, shut your eyes again and simply shake your head, very slowly, from side to side. You are too overwhelmed (or bored) to speak.

Alienated Film Boy
(*Royalus withcheesum*)

Diet:

Nest Type:

Intake:

Foraging Technique:

Plumage: Cigarette perpetually dangling from lips or fingertips (when it is absent, boy frantically pats self down looking for pack). Slim-cut black jeans worn, with ruffled pastel tuxedo shirt if he's feeling "ironic," with a Sundance T-shirt if he's feeling "serious." Converse low-tops (red or black).

Habitat: Video stores (foreign section), wee alternative theater, John Woo film festival. Shooting in the park near the university (cheap student-actor labor, easy access to pilfered equipment) or on a cobblestoned street downtown (atmosphere! atmosphere!). At magazine stand, where he is irresistibly drawn to yet repulsed by all articles about Quentin Tarantino.

Feeding Habits: The Hamburglar is his friend.

Sexual Display: Dresses the same whether he is on the prowl or currently mated—to change his look would be uncool and pretentious (not to mention expensive). Strikes up conversation (usually

about "directors who sell out") with girls in line at the artsy theater for the new Robert Rodriguez or Gregg Araki film. Or sits in café, very publicly crossing out/rewriting script. Despite his professed postmodernism, he may engage in the very premodern gambit of approaching attractive young women and saying "Are you an actress?"

Agonistic Display: When others discuss Tarantino and his "imitators," the Alienated Film Boy goes ballistic. All in his vicinity will be flecked with spittle as he rants maniacally about stealing shots and arrogance and overexposure. He often can be soothed by frequent assurances of his own superior brilliance, coupled with applications of the word "Fellini-esque."

Courtship Behavior: Brings you previously viewed tapes from his day job as a video store clerk. Lets you read his script. Discusses use of tracking shot in *Goodfellas*.

Mating Ritual: Sees everything as if through a camera lens, so his seduction tends toward the stagey. He may even favor silk sheets (though again, if he is in irony mode, leopard print or *Star Wars* sheets are more likely). He caresses your face in a theatrical way, and lets his eyes travel, cameralike, from your feet to your head and back down. He may physically pick you up and move you into a more "cinematic" position, which can prove unnerving in the heat of the moment.

Mating Call: "You look just like Anita Ekberg in *La Dolce Vita*."

Heavy-Lidded Jazz Aficionado
(*Notatus caeruleus*)

Diet: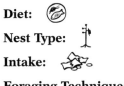

Nest Type:

Intake:

Foraging Technique:

Plumage: In books and films, the species is usually seen in black turtleneck, goatee, beret, dangling cigarette, and bongos. Nowadays he may be wearing chinos and Jack Purcell sneakers, or a T-shirt he bought at a rave with a psychedelic Buddha on it, or mini-dreds, cowrie shell earrings and baggy trou. He may be white or black. In short, this species has evolved tremendously and cross-breeds with several other species.

Habitat: Leafing through jazz collection in record store; jazz club (Village Vanguard, Blue Note, Birdland, Giant Step); museum exhibits devoted to the history of the subject; jazz discussion groups on the Internet; garage sales, looking for some forgotten classic relegated to vinyl; paging through club listings in alternative paper. The serious spotter would do well to attend shows by Doc Cheatham, Lionel Hampton, David Murray, Roy

Hargrove, Joshua Redman, Christian McBride, Herbie Hancock, Max Roach, McCoy Tyner, Freddie Hubbard.

Feeding Habits: Knows how to work the music charge versus minimum. If he can't work it to his advantage, he eats late at night, after the show, at a nearby greasy spoon (finds tuna melts pan-fried in rancid oil and coffee in cups with lipstick traces on them romantic) or, if he's feeling flush, at a jazz cabaret or swanky oak bar.

Alternative: Embracing the outsider nature of the art form, he may choose to go out for Thai, Ethiopian, Spanish, Cuban, Burmese, or Vietnamese food.

Sexual Display: Most Heavy-Lidded Jazz Aficionados are musicians themselves. If he's a pianist, he shows you his reach. If he's a sax player, he offers to demonstrate his fingering. If he's a drummer, he twirls his stick. If he's a bass player, he plucks his strings for you. If he's a trumpet player, he offers to show you how he blows. (Note: Trumpet players are the best kissers.)

Agonistic Display: Existentialist bent. Doesn't matter if he is provoked. It all means nothing. Dig the crazy beats.

Courtship Behavior: Can play you records for hours. Miles, Diz, Coltrane, Dex. (Or if he's an alternative jazz boy, John Zorn and anything recorded live at the Knitting Factory.) The former takes you out to hear all kinds of music, embracing hip-hop hybrids, modern Latino/Cubano/Africano/gypsy influences, classical European traditions and R&B stepsiblings. The latter has strict traditionalist standards: the only living composer he is comfortable with is Wynton Marsalis, and only barely.

Mating Ritual: Good jazz unleashes the powerful libidinal impulses of the id that the uptight superego of bourgeois culture wants to repress. Expect to hear sinuous horns, intricately weaving melodies, a thumping rhythm, a throbbing fast tempo, a heavy beat, complex harmonies, and an urgent sliding drive.

Afterward, he smokes a cigarette.

Mating Call: (Nodding) "Mmm hmmm. Mmmm hmmm."

Smooth 'n' Oily Lounge Act
(*Igottabeme crooner*)

Diet: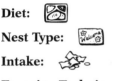

Nest Type:

Intake:

Foraging Technique:

Plumage: Ruffled tuxedo shirt (pastel a possibility), polyester formalwear. Or silky shirt worn unbuttoned to below sternum, gold chains nestled amidst the manly hairs. Tight, narrow-legged trousers. Overlong hair, styled to be poufy on top or combed over (toupee also a possibility) to disguise incipient baldness. When not performing, wears dark, tight jeans and silky shirt or polo shirt. Oversized watch (when consulting it, hums "You've got no time for me, you've got big things to do, well my sweet chickadee, I've got hot news for you . . .")

Habitat: Onstage at hotel or motel watering hole. Headlining at the Venus de Milo lounge. Golf course. Vegas. Renting *Ocean's Eleven*.

Feeding Habits: Red meat: rare sirloin, chops, filet mignon, rib-eyes. Cholesterol thing is a bunch of hooey. Scotch, neat. Martini, up. Black coffee, the morning after.

Sexual Display: Spots attractive blonde in a strappy little jersey number in the front row. Extra hip wiggle during the Tom Jones medley. Winks during "Come Fly with Me." Makes bedroom eyes during "Muskrat Love." Takes it down an octave in an attempt to sound more like Barry White.

Agonistic Display: When heckled, says, "What happens when siblings marry, ladies and gentlemen!" When told his act needs some work, says, "When Frank caught my act in Atlantic City, he said he wouldn't change a thing." When told he sounds like a cat in heat, says, "Wayne Newton, a close personal friend, would not be happy to hear you say that."

Courtship Behavior: Takes you to restaurants with red banquettes, supercilious waiters, and overcooked vegetables. Takes you to the Stardust Lounge for cocktails and to the revolving restaurant on the roof of the big hotel for dinner. Takes you on a weekend jaunt to the casino, where he gives you quarters for the slots and expects you to clutch his arm and squeal while he plays blackjack.

Mating Ritual: Points to his own eyes with the index and middle fingers of one hand. Intones, "See these eyes, baby? These eyes don't lie. These eyes see the most incredible, seductive, feminine woman they have ever seen until this moment. I need you, baby. Save me. Save me from myself." Actual sex act completed in 18.8 seconds.

Mating Call: "Ladies and gentlemen, put your hands together for my girlfriend, the Most Beautiful Girl in the World! All right."

Field Notes: Species pats behinds of cocktail waitresses.

Snarling Gangsta Rapper
(*Lass lassie pooch*)

Diet:

Nest Type:

Intake:

Foraging Technique:

Plumage: When this guide went to press, plumage consisted of head wraps; baggy, low-slung canvas work gear; navy and black tonal palettes; gold jewelry or Afrocentric medallions; work boots. The species molts frequently, however, and changes its plumage often enough so that suburban mack daddy wannabes must be constantly shifting and heading to the mall in an attempt to evolve in pace with the alpha males of the species.

Habitat: At performances of fellow artists, nodding head supportively if artist is on same record label or sneering derisively if artist is on different label. Visiting his mama or grandmama back in the 'hood. Dance club, basking in adoration. Cruising. Boxing matches.

Feeding Habits: Mama's home cooking whenever possible. Fast food when it isn't. Good restaurant soul food when there's time. Secret hidden passion for Froot Loops.

Sexual Display: Hooded stare full of appreciation and meaning. Standard modus operandi: Get member of posse to ask cute girl at concert if she wants to come party backstage afterward. Or swagger up to female at club, casually, no big thing. Say, "What up." Wait for female to coo, make big eyes, and climb aboard the he-train.

Agonistic Display: Attempts to avoid confrontation whenever possible. Why front when you can represent? If, however, he does not receive his due props in course, after keeping it on the d-l for as long as possible, he seeks not to be playing his own self and calls on his peeps for backup.

Courtship Behavior: Seeks to surprise female by behaving in counterpoint to his hard image, by taking her to amusement parks and sappy movies, bringing her mink teddy bears and velvet boxes of chocolate. May, however, sing songs to her about freekin her in every way.

Mating Ritual: Waterbed. Maneuvers female over to it by crooning in her ear, again in opposition to his image, the latest mellifluous, soulful, soaring Jodeci number or a tried-and-true R&B hit that has worked for eons. Does not seek merely to get over, but rather to bowl her over. Considers sexual stamina a personal holy grail: after initial courtship, foreplay may be abbreviated, but the duration of the penetrative act itself is not.

Mating Call: Tells you you are "mad," "deep," "fresh," or "on the real." (Female should smile demurely and appreciatively.)

Pissy Pierced Punk
(*AAAAAARGH eeeeeauhhhcccchh huh huh huh*)

Diet:

Nest Type:

Intake:

Foraging Technique:

Plumage: Festive tattoos. Enough piercings to set off airport metal detector. Hair in many colors not found in nature. Music-producing equipment (i.e., plugged in to Walkman or Discman, or carrying boom box). Emaciated, terrible posture. Rancid T-shirt with sleeves ripped off. Belt covered with studs or spikes. If Punk is old-school, may sport mohawk hairdo, crafted with gel and Elmer's glue. If you do spy a mohawk, be aware that you are viewing a nearly extinct subspecies and approach it with concern and care. Speak to it softly.

Habitat: Drugstore, over by the Manic Panic hair dye. The Gauntlet piercing emporium (note, though, that some Punks do not find the piercing experience to be authentic unless it is conducted in an alleyway with an unsterilized needle from a travel sewing kit that's fallen on the ground a few times), dark club, local heroin den, parts of town your mother warned you about. However, the suburbanite need not despair of spotting a Punk—she is likely to spy multitudes of tiny suburban Punk boys hovering around the local record outlet buying Green Day albums and peeing surreptitiously in mall flowerbeds.

Feeding Habits: Hostess snack products, cheap beer, pizza, heroin, speed, cold medications (in bulk).

Sexual Display: Gropes attractive female in the mosh pit (alternatively, the gentlemanly punk rescues attractive female from being groped in the mosh pit). When he wipes his sweat on a female, it means he is seeking an introduction.

Agonistic Display: Hurls entire body against hostile male. Sneers. Spits. Vomits on Other's shoes.

Courtship Behavior: Shyly proffers tickets to underground show he has begged doorman friend for for weeks. Offers to pierce you. Gives you singles by bands with names like "Dahmer's Refrigerator" and "Butt Hate."

Mating Ritual: Shows up at your house unannounced. Pokes through your refrigerator. Watches TV with you, mocking the various shows. Goes through your record collection, commenting unfavorably on it. When you are both on your knees looking at old Sex Pistols albums, he kisses you.

Mating Call: "Beer?"

Field Notes: Can you hear the Pissy Pierced Punk in the wild? Listen for a falling "Ramo-o-o-o-o-ones" flute tone, or repeated "bite me, bite me, bite me" whistle. In midflight (airborne in the mosh pit) listen for a soft "bollocks, bollocks, yeah" or a high, sibilant "you suck!"

The Pissy Pierced Punk may have any of
the following distinguishing markings:

PIERCING HOMUNCULUS

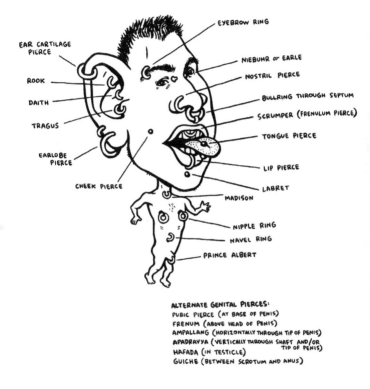

EYEBROW RING

EAR CARTILAGE PIERCE

ROOK

DAITH

TRAGUS

EARLOBE PIERCE

CHEEK PIERCE

NIEBUHR or EARLE

NOSTRIL PIERCE

BULLRING THROUGH SEPTUM

SCRUMPER (FRENULUM PIERCE)

TONGUE PIERCE

LIP PIERCE

LABRET

MADISON

NIPPLE RING

NAVEL RING

PRINCE ALBERT

ALTERNATE GENITAL PIERCES:
PUBIC PIERCE (AT BASE OF PENIS)
FRENUM (ABOVE HEAD OF PENIS)
AMPALLANG (HORIZONTALLY THROUGH TIP OF PENIS)
APADRAVYA (VERTICALLY THROUGH SHAFT AND/OR TIP OF PENIS)
HAFADA (IN TESTICLE)
GUICHE (BETWEEN SCROTUM AND ANUS)

Note: The Prince Albert, a ring through the tip of the penis, is probably the most common genital pierce. Victorian gentlemen used it to secure their manhood to the right or left pants leg, thereby minimizing the telltale bulge.

Alternative Rock Boy
(*Cobainus howlum*)

Diet:

Nest Type:

Intake:

Foraging Technique:

Plumage: Lank hair hanging in face, battered army jacket, ripped knee-length shorts, decomposing 1982 Ramones T-shirt (variants: fetching frock, body paint), guitar case, repetitive twitching or strumming motions with fingers when idle, nonexistent muscle tone, black eye (run-in with Courtney Love).

Habitat: Pawn shops selling vintage amps, suburban garages, dank, unventilated clubs, seedy record stores (species does not thrive in gleaming Coconuts and Wherehouse outlets), yard sales (poring over crates of Carpenters and Eagles LPs in the hopes of finding some hidden Big Star classic).

Feeding Habits: Frozen waffles, Rolling Rock in the bottle, heroin.

Sexual Display: Eye contact from the stage. Stage dives into female's corpus. Gets stickers with band name printed on them, sticks them on passing females. Additional gel.

Agonistic Display: "Your sound is tired" are incendiary words to the *Cobainus howlum*'s ears. Expect fisticuffs. Because much of his music is grounded in aggression, beer throwing may ensue during shows. The more melodic Alternative Rock Boys let their hostilities out through lyrics about stupid people they have known. When testosterone is running particularly high, the species may incite aggressive moshing.

Courtship Behavior: Buys you a Parliament eight-track (message: "I am ironic, yet sincere"). Lets you touch his record collection. (At this point, you may murmur something about the "humanizing" qualities of vinyl.) Writes a song with your name in it. Asks you to feed his cat when he's playing out. Invites you to watch him practice. (Bring a book.)

Mating Ritual: The more melodically inclined Alternative Rock Boys are also the more romantic members of the species. Those who prefer a harder sound are also more likely to have their courtship impressions formed by excessive MTV exposure. Convinced that girls are "supposed to" throw themselves at boys in bands, they are less likely to engage in gentle seduction techniques. This means they are more likely to rip your clothes off, do their business, and start snoring.

Mating Call: "So, like, if you wanna come I can probably get you on the list."

Field Notes: Conversing with Soulful Music Boy: If Soulful Music Boy is droning on about some obscure band and you wish to seem alert, say simply, "Their first release was really groundbreaking." You do not need a clue as to who they are. Boy will go off on how, God, you are so right, listen to the

bass line, you are so perceptive, they've totally be-
trayed the fans since then (i.e., they signed with a
major label).

Discerning the evolutionary weaknesses of a
given Soulful Musician Boy: Say, "Actually, I play
bass in a girl band." If he sneers, he is weak mating
material. If he perks right up, he's a keeper. This test
is as reliable as the Pythagorean theorem.

Acerbic Bipolar Novelist
(*Burroughs kerouacum*)

Diet:

Nest Type:

Intake:

Foraging Technique:

Plumage: Tattered paperback (often *The Brothers Karamazov* or *Foucault's Pendulum*) in back pocket of Levi's or brown corduroys, which hug his cute little butt. Bulky sweater (believes he has poor circulation, as this is very glamorous sounding). Small notebook. Old-fashioned fountain pen (bar mitzvah gift).

Habitat: Alone at table in café with notebook and Camels or *Gravity's Rainbow* and highlighter. Rundown studio apartment in shabby neighborhood, with bookshelves consisting of unfinished pine boards propped up on cinderblocks. Lumpy futon. If possessor of trust fund, may live in ritzy, yuppie section of town he professes to despise. Newsstand, reading the *New Yorker* and sneering. Cemetery.

Feeding Habits: Caffeine. Grilled-cheese sandwiches made on clothes iron.

Sexual Display: Hovers near the Anaïs Nin section of the bookstore. When attractive, haunted-looking young woman picks up a volume of erotica or the diaries, swoops in for the kill.

Agonistic Display: Many things set him off. The word of a huge advance for the next novel of a writer he considers marginal. A rejection letter from an obscure literary quarterly in rural Arkansas. A price increase at Kinko's Copies. When threatened by the success of a rival, he grits his teeth and recites the Clive James poem "The Book of My Enemy Has Been Remaindered."

Courtship Behavior: Takes you out for espressos (you pay). Takes you to lectures and readings by famous authors (you pay). During lecture or reading by famous author, slumps in his chair, rolls eyes, snorts, occasionally mutters something like "nice mixed metaphor, dude." After lecture or reading by famous author, invariably picks a fight with you. (He refuses to see this pattern.) Asks you to read his work, stares raptly at you as you do so.

Mating Ritual: Starts using many strange adjectives to describe your mystical, hypnotic beauty. Objectifies body parts you didn't know were attractive—your inner wrist, your ears ("shell-like"?), the underside of your jaw. Reads Pablo Neruda's sonnets or Harold Brodkey's borderline-pornographic short stories aloud to you in a husky voice.

Mating Call: "Have you read *Tropic of Cancer?*"

Field Notes: Ambivalence and the Acerbic Novelist: The writer's mating dance involves a hugely passionate beginning—overheated letters on beautiful handmade paper and insane, beard-burn-inducing sex—followed by the big chill. This species cannot commit, because the bourgeois monogamy thing would extinguish his creative spark. Thus he is a master at the ritual song: It's not you, it's me; you deserve someone better; I'm very damaged; I'm working on it; etc. If you leave, he will soon bombard you with pleas to return. If you return, the pattern of chase and flee, chase and flee, will continue until you are as frazzled and high-strung as a blue-throated hummingbird (*Lampornis clemenciae*).

Starving Disaffected Art Male
(*Piccasus basquiatum*)

Diet: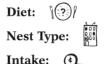

Nest Type:

Intake:

Foraging Technique:

Plumage: Endearingly paint-splashed or redolent of darkroom chemicals. Surgically attached sketch pad. Piercing stare alternating with blasé eye-rolling.

Habitat: Art supply stores, clucking tongue with disgust at price of cadmium red. Park bench, biting lower lip and sketching like a fiend (babe magnet behavior). Galleries (stands motionless in front of single painting for twenty minutes, then theatrically storms out with tears in his eyes).

Feeding Habits: Goes to art openings, sneers at the work, stuffs face with free Brie, leaves.

Sexual Display: Approaches beautiful, dark, thin women and announces, "You look like a Modigliani." (If woman has curly hair, a Botticelli. If woman is curvy and pink-cheeked, a Renoir. If woman is blonde, a Titian.)

Agonistic Display: Not a pack animal. Loudly disparages the talent of all other art boys. Puts his enemies into his art (incorporating mutilated photographs of them into multimedia compositions, or simply titling an abstract painting *Chris Kalb Has Like No Talent Compared to Me*).

Courtship Behavior: Gets you to pose for him "undraped" (i.e., *naked*), because it's art.

Mating Ritual: Enacts erotic artist-model scenarios from *Lust for Life, Camille Claudel,* Bon Jovi videos. The Starving Disaffected Art Male is tactile, which makes him a sensitive lover. Also, he has had experience waiting for clay to dry. This makes him patient when the wily female orgasm is elusive.

Mating Call: "You are one of the few people who could comprehend what my work is trying to say."

Field Notes: Dating the *Piccasus basquiatum* because you hope his work will appreciate in value and you'll end up a millionairess is a very dicey bet.

Family:
Gainfully Employed

Patient Pediatrician	*Sympatheticus georgeclooney*
Charming and Useful Dermatologist	*Hypoallergenicus alphahydroxy*
Possibly Judgmental Psychiatrist	*Couchus sigmund*
Corporate Lawyer Guy	*Cochranus armani*
Ugly-Shoe-Wearing Public Interest Guy	*Nebbish virtuus*
Aggro Investment Banker	*Avaricius rollover*
Hearty Salesman Guy	*Assertivus dalecarnegie*
Witty Advertising Exec	*Seductus product*
Competent Stolid Accountant	*Hohum hohum*
Patriarchal Yet Nurturing College Professor	*Schlumpus intellect*
Socially Awkward/Possibly Deep Computer Geek	*Cyberdorkus perpetuum*
Bitter Freeloading Journalist	*Steno conspirasus*
High-Strung Chef	*Julius child*
Capable Electrician/ Telephone Installer	*Birdona wire*
Smoldering Forest Ranger	*Yogius smoky*
Wiry Housepainter	*Cannibis latex*
Bemuscled Construction Worker	*Leerus oglus*

About Gainfully Employed Boys

Some Gainfully Employed males gain their entire sense of identity from their jobs (this causes problems in the current era of downsizing, but that is another book). Other Gainfully Employeds do not view their work as their primary source of self-identification. In their innermost heart of hearts, they still see themselves as musicians, football stars, swanky Lotharios. They have a desk, but the desk does not define them. Therefore, you might wish to look at the Artsy, Athletic, and Casual sections for insight into a particular Gainfully Employed's behavior. Your male may, for example, contain some genetic elements of an Athletic that have not been fully weeded out through exposure to the workaday world. Evolution takes time. Individual office-drone males may not relinquish their dreams of playing for the New Jersey Nets in spite of the fact that they are 5'8" with no jump shot to speak of. They may fantasize about jamming with Eddie Van Halen even as their hairlines recede and their ability to remember lyrics fades. It's endearing.

Patient Pediatrician
(*Sympatheticus georgeclooney*)

Diet:

Nest Type:

Intake:

Foraging Technique:

Plumage: Coloration: dappled with drool and spit-up. The *Sympatheticus georgeclooney*'s clothes are designed for mobility, letting him chase a recalcitrant five-year-old through a waiting room, get down to eye level for a heart-to-heart with a toddler, and crawl around on the floor searching for a stethoscope hurled by an outraged infant. In his soft sweaters and shirts in pleasing colors, he looks approachable, unthreatening, nonjarring—pretty much the visual equivalent of Ritalin.

Habitat: If you have a child, sightings are likely. If you have no child, you might borrow one. When not on the job, the Patient Pediatrician enjoys spending time with people who have successfully completed puberty. Look for him in conversation-oriented activities like softball games and benefit parties, enjoying such adult concepts as irony, multisyllabic words, casual swearing, and the absence of Barney.

Feeding Habits: *Sympatheticus* has that love of good food common to those in the medical profession, but he has one particular occupational hazard: cravings for brightly colored, synthetic bad-for-you foods. His job makes him familiar with sugary neon fruit leather, cereals with marshmallows in terrifying hues, cupcakes, and gelatin worms. Do not shame him for this predilection. When a new movie-themed comestible appears on your supermarket shelf, bring it to his nest and watch him examine it delightedly, like a bowerbird with a bright shiny object.

Sexual Display: See *Hypoallergenicus alphahydroxy*—for the *Sympatheticus georgeclooney* too the downy white coat is a sexual signifier. Outside the medical setting, he is likely to wear baseball caps and Converse low-tops, which is attributable to the fact that he himself is still childish (hence his attraction to the field in the first place), and that he has processed the evolutionary lesson that many women find boyish men adorable.

Agonistic Display: The pediatrician is not one for flamboyant agonistic displays. This is because he is indisputably so high on the food chain—his profession is nearly universally regarded as making him desirable mating material—that he seldom becomes threatened by other males. He regards them from his lofty aerie with humor and slight pity. In addition, coping day in and day out with the irrationality, pouting, and stubbornness of children gives him a nearly female understanding of adult male behavior.

Courtship Behavior: Communication is his specialty. He is charming and attentive during courtship, often trying to ascertain what kinds of activities are preferred by the female and engaging in them with her. Yet with this behavior—ornithologists call it mirroring—his inner self remains elusive. Do you like golf? He likes golf. Do you like Thai food? He likes Thai food. This attribute can be a delight or a profound annoyance.

Mating Ritual: The pediatrician has read the women's magazines in his waiting room. He knows about candlelight and eye contact. His body-language-reading skills have been honed by days spent trying to read two-year-olds' minds. He undresses the female as if unwrapping a valuable present, lavishing attention on her entire body, not just her breasts and crotch. He is incredibly verbal and attuned to your words and gestures. Again, this can be delicious or it can make you feel that his true desires are madly elusive.

Mating Call: "You remind me of the yellow Power Ranger." (Note: Apparently a compliment.)

Field Notes: Pediatricians have the best social skills of all the medical specialties. Brain surgeons and orthopedists have the worst, and are often arrogant, nonfun workaholics to boot. Radiologists are often cynical opportunists with the souls of tradesmen who entered medicine for the hefty paycheck and nebulous desire to "help people" without getting their hands bloodstained. As for psychiatrists and dermatologists, see the next two listings.

Charming and
Useful Dermatologist
(*Hypoallergenicus alphahydroxy*)

Diet: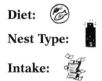

Nest Type:

Intake:

Foraging Technique:

Plumage: Usually fit and dapper, with scrupulously clean fingernails. At work, may sport pleated dress trousers, white shirt with the sleeves boyishly rolled up, tie. Seldom wears jacket, as it constrains him in his athletic dash from boil-lancing to dermabrasion to comedo-extraction. When seeing patients, he usually wears a lab coat as protection from propulsive pus when popping pustules.

Habitat: Your greatest likelihood of a sighting is in his office (funny how that works), which is unhappily when you yourself are at your least presentable—e.g., with a mammoth zit or a raging case of eczema. Thus you may prefer to take your binoculars to alternate dermatologist-stuffed habitats. Dermatologists frequent singles bars. They have nice golden retrievers (aka babe magnets) that they take for walks in the park. Since dermatologists are

frequently attracted to glamor, the hip bar of the moment or the must-see new movie is a good place to hunt.

Feeding Habits: The dermatologist often eats on the run, since he must pack the patients in to earn his daily bread. For lunch, he has gourmet carryout, a bag lunch of last night's grilled tuna (reincarnated on sourdough with olive tapenade), a salad from the deli . . . but heaven forfend, no fast food. Yes, most of us know that french-fry grease doesn't actually cause pimples, but what if one of the poor deluded souls who still believes that old wives' tale happens to be his patient and happens to see him in Burger World?

Sexual Display: When hunting for a mate, the dermatologist keeps his white coat immaculate, starched and pressed (he believes the white coat, in tandem with the medical degree on the wall, triggers estrus in the female). He grooms himself with extra applications of moisturizer and alcohol-free toner.

Agonistic Display: The dermatologist picked this job because he reaps the prestige and salary of a medical degree with the hours of a beautician. Of course he is defensive about not being perceived as a "real doctor." Thus he is deeply threatened by males who say jocularly, "You went to med school to pop zits?" and may lash out in response—with, for example, "I think that's a carcinoma on your nose" or "If you didn't drink so much, you wouldn't have so many broken capillaries."

Courtship Behavior: When courting, the dermatologist presents the female with tiny bottles of cleanser (freebies from manufacturers). He asks her to dinner—dermatologists are usually fine and glib conversationalists, accustomed to looking alert and saying "uh huh" without actually listening—or to medical conventions in exotic locales (though he orders her not to sit in the sun, as it will make him look bad) or to the movies, where he delights in whispering which actresses have had chemical peels. In late-stage courtship, he may offer her a free collagen injection.

Mating Ritual: As the dermatologist caresses the female's face, he tells her he does not even see her fine lines and wrinkles. As he kisses her lips, he tells her that they are remarkably soft, though she should be using lip balm with SPF 15 every day, even under lipstick. As he nibbles teasingly down her body, he informs her that she should shave with, not against, the direction of the hair.

Mating Call: "Can I exfoliate you?"

Field Notes: The dermatologist is frequently surrounded by gorgeous, well-preserved, self-absorbed women. For this reason, if you are attempting to lure the specimen, it may be more strategic from a mating standpoint to be natural. No makeup, no beauty obsessiveness. He may well be so baffled by your exoticism that he is won.

Possibly Judgmental Psychiatrist
(*Couchus sigmund*)

Diet:

Nest Type:

Intake:

Foraging Technique:

Plumage: If he's a full-on Freudian, look for an expressionless face, neatly trimmed facial hair, utterly neutral clothing, and unreadable body language. Freudians are the dun-colored peahens of the psychiatric world. Other schools of therapeutic thought display greater variation in plumage. But why are you so concerned about how he dresses? Does this have something to do with your childhood?

Habitat: Psychiatrists are often attracted to cultural offerings, like museums, ballets, and performances of *Der Rosenkavelier*. They may also frequent exquisite restaurants, wine tastings, cooking classes, gourmet shops, and the supermarket aisle that contains peppercorns.

Feeding Habits: The psychiatrist's appreciation for elegance is reflected in his love of fine food. The perfectly seared salmon, the artfully arranged

sushi, the veal chop seasoned just so—all these are the psychiatrist's attempt to convince himself that the world is a controllable, peaceful place, so unlike the unruly human brain.

Sexual Display: Combs the biscotti crumbs out of his beard. Buys a new sweater-vest.

Agonistic Display: Agonistic displays? The psychiatrist doesn't think so. His hostility is very well channeled. He is not threatened by other males because he has a well-integrated sense of self. Anyone who suggests otherwise is probably an id-driven sociopath with bedwetting tendencies.

Courtship Behavior: Tries to impose his cultural will upon you—he thinks dating means traditional activities like plays, concerts, walks in the park. Psychiatrists aren't always the most flexible species in courtship; if he is uncomfortable in a setting or with the company, he will twitch and fidget like a schizophrenic on too much Haldol.

Mating Ritual: Remember that spate of films a few years ago about sexually twisted psychiatrists? It's all true. Look for bondage equipment, harnesses, whips, and dildos in the cabinet by the bed. Either that or he's totally repressed and needs the missionary position and total darkness in order to perform. If he asks you to point out on a stuffed doll where you'd like him to touch you, he may not be comfortable with his sexuality.

Mating Call: "In a certain light, you look just like my mother."

Corporate Lawyer Guy
(*Cochranus armani*)

Diet:

Nest Type:

Intake:

Foraging Technique:

Plumage: Armani suit, don't-fuck-with-me tie, wingtips, briefcase, haircut so sharp you could slice cheese with it.

Habitat: Gleaming office tower, expensive lunch joints where he schmoozes clients, courthouse (if he's a trial guy). Weekends, he exercises (the *Cochranus* is the determinedly blank-faced one over at the bench press or the insanely competitive one on the squash court), takes two-day getaways to warmer climes, ski slopes, and beachfront property. Also drops off his laundry (extra starch, thanks) and tries on new suits. The deluded lawyer may view himself as a rebel in a corporate body, causing him to hang out at trendy, slightly seedy downtown bars in the hopes of meeting a funky, pierced, sexually scary girl.

Feeding Habits: Only eats where he can hear the comforting call, "Would you like some fresh ground pepper?"

Sexual Display: Most common sexual display is the ritualistic waving of the Gold or Platinum Card. The *Cochranus* must put in hellish hours at his firm, leaving late nights for mate-seeking. Frequents upscale charity events, where he drinks single-malt scotch and scans the room like a vulture searching for carrion.

Agonistic Display: Wields legalistic Latin jargon like a club.

Courtship Behavior: Accustomed to thinking in billable hours, the *Cochranus* budgets only small blocks of time for a given date. He frequently "multitasks," trying to get as much accomplished as possible at once. A frequent second-year-law-student gambit is taking the willing female to a corporate picnic or evening out with one of the firm's partners and the partner's wife: a deadly dull but impressively expensive evening.

Mating Ritual: Puts Sade or Billie Holiday on the CD player—he's a classicist. Enjoys the process of undressing a woman—it reminds him of unwrapping a present, which is pleasantly associated in his mind with accruing possessions.

Mating Call: "How do you feel about prenuptual agreements?"

Field Notes: The *Cochranus*'s taste in mates in quite diverse. Certain members of the species seem drawn to women in fields as unlike their own as possible—artists, punk rockers, dancers. Others prefer the feminine plumage of Talbot's sweater, headband, and blonde bob, confident that the most "presentable" female will convey the most status in the dominance hierarchy (aka "the firm").

Ugly-Shoe-Wearing
Public Interest Guy
(*Nebbish virtuus*)

Diet:

Nest Type:

Intake:

Foraging Technique:

Plumage: Timex. Battered loafers. Soft-sided briefcase. Tie bought from street-corner vendor for four dollars. Carrying the latest Robert Coles or Henry Louis Gates book. Perpetual haunted look.

Habitat: Jail (note: not the most hospitable habitat for female ethologists), courthouse, community organizing meetings, anti–death penalty rallies, panel discussions on fair housing, ACLU lectures.

Feeding Habits: Egg salad with Miracle Whip, eaten at his desk. Dolphin-safe tuna on white bread (note: does not mean he has any problems with black bread, which is a perfectly wonderful bread that is equal in every way to white bread). Tagamet.

Sexual Display: Takes out personal ads that start "Sensitive Seinfeld lookalike seeks . . ."

Agonistic Display: A shouter. Aggressive vocalizations asserting his special understanding of the problems plaguing the legal system, the environment,

death row inmates, the underclass, the criminal justice system in general. Can sing his song of injustice for many, many hours, simply raising the volume when a male from a different species (or often, the same species) attempts to disagree or engage in a duet.

Courtship Behavior: Brings the female articles from socialist newspapers about the plight of the migrant worker. Indicates willingness to be monogamous (this species is less flighty than many others)—calls when he says he'll call, displays little fear of commitment, as long as the female does not attempt to come between him and his labors on behalf of all humanity.

Mating Ritual: Introduces you to his mother.

Mating Call: "Wanna come to the public transit authority's open hearing about the fare hike?"

Field Notes: Field calls the female can try:

1. "Free Mumia!"
2. "My cat is named Thurgood."
3. "I heard John Grisham cheated on the bar."
4. "I used to be a waitress in Alan Dershowitz's kosher deli, and oh, the stories I could tell."
5. "Gee, I wish someone could explain the history of the insanity defense to me . . ."

Aggro Investment Banker
(*Avaricius rollover*)

Diet:

Nest Type:

Intake:

Foraging Technique:

Plumage: Hugo Boss double-breasted suit with intimidating shoulder pads—he looks like an inverted wedge. Shoes as shiny as Christmas tree ornaments. Excellent skin; he sees a facialist. *Investor's Business Daily* tucked beneath his personal-trainer-buffed triceps.

Habitat: Climate-controlled office with an expansive view of the entire city. When his secretary is at lunch, he stands at the window and growls, "I am Master of all I survey!" Dines at expensive but stodgy restaurants. Weekends, frequents Sharper Image and upscale sporting-goods stores, golf courses, polo fields.

Feeding Habits: Extremely carnivorous.

Sexual Display: Primary sexual display is the exposure of the cash wad. The crisp, crackling sound of bills being casually flicked off the wad is widely believed to trigger sperm production.

Agonistic Display: His shoulder pads stiffen at the sight of liberal wussies who are opposed to the capital gains tax cut. When angered, his voice gets louder and louder and he bounces on the tips of his Bruno Magli–clad toes. Likes the idea of a fistfight, since he pays the personal trainer so goddamn much, but would never actually have one. And he just had his nails buffed.

Courtship Behavior: Expects a return on his investment. In other words, if you don't sleep with him by the third date you're history. Then again, he may see the value of a commodity that is difficult to attain, which would mean he doesn't even try to kiss you until the third date.

Mating Ritual: Clicks a button on the remote of his sleek, black home entertainment console, causing the seductive sounds of Anita Baker to flood the room. Puts aside his glass of Moët. Kisses you. Undresses you, silently noting designer labels in your clothing as he goes. Undresses self, down to the Sulka cotton boxers. Lays you down on Pratesi sheets. Is finished in five minutes. Every time.

Mating Call: "I don't want my wife to work."

Hearty Salesman Guy
(*Assertivus dalecarnegie*)

Diet: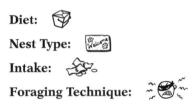

Nest Type:

Intake:

Foraging Technique:

Plumage: Travel-weight suit, shirt collar slightly damp from constant exertion of charm. Packed briefcase (with lock) full of everything he needs for a day of putting customers first, shooting straight, establishing credibility, staying in touch, feeding the pipeline, and being flexible and responsive to individual customers' needs!

Habitat: Always on the go, assisting customers and insuring their satisfaction. Look for him on airplanes and in car-rental offices. When not mobile, he's on the phone. Sometimes he's mobile and on the phone—he's often surgically attached to his cellular.

Feeding Habits: He's a dynamic entrepreneurial spirit on the run, eating breakfast bars, pita roll-ups, and beef jerky as he goes!

Sexual Display: Only goes tieless when he is on the prowl, looking elaborately casual in his open-

collared shirt and Dockers. Frequents singles bars, muttering pep talks to himself. ("Think persistence and strategy. Look for opportunities and needs and capitalize. Don't beat your head against a wall. Reposition yourself and keep moving.") When asked what he does for a living, answers, "I am a sales professional who addresses customer concerns in a dynamic, interactive way that maximizes results."

Agonistic Display: Challenges rivals directly: Who has more frequent-flier miles?

Courtship Behavior: Enjoys excrutiatingly fun dating activities—bowling, horseback riding, apple-picking—during which he keeps asking heartily, "Havin' fun, babe?" Takes a special female as his date to a motivational training seminar in Hawaii or Cancún, where she may feel like an escapee from a Tony Robbins infomercial.

Mating Ritual: He maximizes your arousal potential with soft music and dim lights. He utilizes his best assets—his smile, his left profile—to get you into the bedroom. He authorizes you to put your pleasure in his hands. (In addition, expect him to employ nouns as verbs; e.g., "Honey, I want to transition this relationship.")

Mating Call: "Sweetie, when you're with me, you can think *win-win.*"

Field Notes: Once his language has been learned, the *Assertivus dalecarnegie* is easily manipulated. The evolutionarily savvy female can create and use incentive programs to get him to do what she wants. Motivate him with praise; for example, "Honey, you're an achiever! You better go out and get some more bagels!"

Witty Advertising Exec
(*Seductus product*)

Diet:

Nest Type:

Intake:

Foraging Technique:

Plumage: Depends on the client. If he is selling sneakers, he dresses like he just stopped by the office on the way to shoot hoops. If he is selling gin, he dresses like a 1930s *New Yorker* illustration, in a tweed suit and playful, graphic tie. In any case, count on a reverence for fashion and pop culture bordering on the fanatical.

Habitat: During the day, spends hours soaking up the culture he needs to understand for his job. You can spot him studying magazine after magazine at the huge newsstand. At night, he spends time in snazzy boîtes and groovy bars, or staying at home in his ironic yet slavishly decorated apartment (vintage advertising posters or framed canned fruit labels on the walls) watching **MTV** to see "what the kids are into."

Feeding Habits: Prides himself on his knowledge of food trends. If the gourmet food store is stocking a new imported fruit vinegar, he must possess it, even if he cooks at home about three times a year. He also loathes being perceived as passé, foodwise. If he eats anything once hip but whose coolness is now in question—blackened anything, risotto, crème caramel—he lies awake nights worrying.

Sexual Display: Goes to parties and bars with his fellow ad execs, talking loudly about how his ideas are too breathtakingly radical for the client. Looks around to see if any cute girls have overheard.

Agonistic Display: Loathes the narrow-minded types who force him to put commerce before art. Tries to shock them by dating a model.

Courtship Behavior: Galleries, bars, restaurants, club- and party-hopping, visits to friends with great weekend homes, performances. When courted by the Witty Advertising Exec, be aware that he is orchestrating your date like a commercial. In the frenzied rush of activity, you will not be able to get a handle on what he's really like. This is as he intends. Until he is certain of what you are shopping for, he won't turn on the hard sell.

Mating Ritual: Expect seductive music and a top-of-the-line sound system (controllable by remote, so he won't have to get up and change the CD midmoment). He will not call for three days, because he knows that if he remains elusive, he maintains his mystique. If you think he wants you too much, you will not appreciate him. (Do not try to out-strategize the Witty Advertising Exec. He has had much more practice than you have.)

Mating Call: Just Do It™

Field Notes: In the advertising world, the *Seductus product* is known as a "creative." If you are observing an "account," the subject will have far more in common with the Hearty Salesman Guy and the Competent Stolid Accountant than with its advertising brethren.

Competent Stolid Accountant
(*Hohum hohum*)

Diet: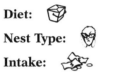

Nest Type:

Intake:

Foraging Technique:

Plumage: As neutral and gray as the plain tit-mouse (*Parus inornatus*). An adequately fitting but not too expensive jacket, trousers that are passable knockoffs of those with more expensive cuts and fabrics, shoes that are neither purple Doc Martens nor Armani wingtips. The *Hohum hohum* blends into the foliage.

Habitat: Office cubicle (or "cube"). Bar frequented by other accountants (members of a given flock tend to vocalize, fly, and look alike—apparently this protects them from predators). Punching numbers (weekly food budget) into calculator on public transportation.

Feeding Habits: The supermarket-brand item is invariably cheaper, but then, there is of course the possibility of greater taste and freshness with the name brand. A formula of cost-effectiveness is therefore necessary: the true cost of the item divided by its added value of pleasure.

Sexual Display: None. The Competent Stolid Accountant in heat is impossible to distinguish from the Competent Stolid Accountant thinking about a spreadsheet.

Agonistic Display: In an office setting, may react to a perceived threat by another male by allowing said male's expense-reimbursement check to languish with Delores in payroll for weeks. He may turn down the male's request for a cash advance for a business trip or tell the male that he has not turned in his petty cash receipts when, in fact, they are sitting in a maliciously shredded little pile in the Accountant's wastebasket.

Courtship Behavior: Sends flowers (1-800-FLOWERS is fairly affordable, and the payoff in goodwill is quite high).

Mating Ritual: As he undresses you, notes the labels in your clothes, sorting them mentally by whites, colors, and needs to be dry-cleaned. After he sees your bathroom, brings you the *Consumer Reports* article debunking costly shampoos.

Mating Call: "You don't balance your checkbook? That's so dangerous, yet so cute!"

Patriarchal Yet Nurturing College Professor
(*Schlumpus intellect*)

Diet:

Nest Type:

Intake:

Foraging Technique:

Plumage: Untidy, overgrown, tufty hair (entices female students who want to "take care of him"). Vintage tweed or corduroy jacket with elbow patches (note: vintage does not mean elegantly antiquated; it means it's been in his closet since 1981 and has too-tight armholes and Bic stains on the sleeve). Blue palms from erasing the dry-erase board with his hands. Food on shirt. Hush Puppies.

Habitat: Roams around college campus looking abstracted and forlorn. During mating season, holds regular office hours (when not mating, can scarcely be troubled to make himself available to students). Eats in undergraduate dining hall to indicate openness to student contact (ahem).

Feeding Habits: Eats in library (brazenly, unlike the surreptitious student eaters), at his desk, and at receptions for visiting Nobel Prize winners, to whom he sucks up. More a grazer than a true eater—occasionally finds lint-covered brownie,

wrapped in napkin, in jacket pocket where it has resided since the last faculty tea. Eats it.

Sexual Display: Crinkles his eyes at the corners with forced charm when he smiles; he knows students find his laugh lines way cute. Carries copies of his own book to show to foxy academic groupies. Invites babes to be his "research assistant."

Agonistic Display: Seething with agonistic hostility. To younger, rising departmental stars, says, "You kids today, coming of age with political correctness, really haven't learned to think for yourselves, have you?" To older, more established academic talents, says, "Well, your critical approach certainly has withstood the test of time, ha ha!"

Courtship Behavior: Takes you to the one "fancy" Italian restaurant in range of campus, where the waitresses roll their eyes as soon as they see him with yet another young woman, though at the time you do not process this, because you are so special and different from all his previous "conquests," whom he has never viewed as his intellectual equal, unlike you, who he clearly values for your fresh insights and untapped depth. Goes browsing in college bookstore with you, handing you titles you absolutely must read if you are to become a true intellectual. Lets you rearrange his index cards and do his photocopying.

Mating Ritual: He finally invites you to his home for tea, wine, or dinner. You sit next to each other on his couch, talking awkwardly about poststructuralism until you say something half-credible and he pretends to be overcome by your brilliance and leans in to kiss you.

Mating Call: "You write with such clarity, so unfettered by theoretical jargon and obfuscated thinking!"

Field Notes: Close observers of the academic scene have stories of professor-student unions that lasted. However, these are so few and far between, many experts assume they are due to some sort of genetic mutation on the part of the *Schlumpus intellect* in question. In most cases, the professor becomes bored/panicky about losing his tenure, or the student slowly realizes she is but one in a long line of young scholars whose lust for knowledge has become confused with lust for the man who imparts it.

Socially Awkward/Possibly Deep Computer Geek
(*Cyberdorkus perpetuum*)

Diet:

Nest Type:

Intake:

Foraging Technique:

Plumage: Most *Cyberdorki* are recognizable by their too-short pants, thick glasses, and fine dusting of dandruff. However, there are two lesser-known subspecies: *Cyberrdorkus techno* enjoys cute hats, oversized clothing, and computer-manufactured music (put a speaker in your window and blast Orbital or Freaky Chakra and he will fly to your sill). *Cyberdorkus mogul* is a nattily dressed, parasitic creature increasingly colonizing the nesting grounds, determined to create mass-market entertainment products in areas where the nerds once roamed free.

Habitat: Desk (der). William Gibson readings. *Star Trek* conventions. Hacker meetings. Raves (*Cyberdorkus techno*). Panels on "Making Your First Million on the Infobahn" (*Cyberdorkus mogul*). Electronic bulletin boards. PC Expo.

Feeding Habits: *Cyberdorkus perpetuum* et *techno:* Lucky Charms, Fruity Pebbles, Peanut But-

ter Cap'n Crunch (bemoans death of Quisp). Techno subset: Twizzlers, SweeTarts, Pixie Stix. *Cyberdorkus mogul:* The trendy cuisine of the moment. Mongolian barbeque? Fugu fish? Boar pasta with white truffle shavings? He's there.

Sexual Display: *Cyberdorkus perpetuum:* Bathes. *Cyberdorkus techno:* Purchases brand-new silver Doc Martens and "Aliens Have Landed" T-shirt. *Cyberdorkus mogul:* Brandishes invite to opening of new Hard Rock Cafe–like cybertheme restaurant.

Agonistic Display: Hacks enemy's credit rating. Taps into enemy's telephone system and sells his calling-card number to expatriate Bangladeshis and devotees of the 1-900-PEEEEEE phone-sex line.

Courtship Behavior: Allots you your own Eudora mailbox. Gives you the number to his alphanumeric pager so you can send him instant email love letters. Calls you "cybergirl" and "modem mama" even after you tell him to cut it out. You have dated for three months before you've even seen him in person.

Mating Ritual: Takes off the Spock ears. Nuzzles your neck. Tells you you look like Agent Scully.

Mating Call (typed on an AOL screen): R U a girl?

Field Notes: The evolutionarily savvy female should consider the advantage of dating a male with very rudimentary social skills. The *Cyberdorkus perpetuum* is eager to please and easy to train. Anecdotal experience indicates that he is more willing to perform oral sex than other males—his childhood fascination with bivalves means he is unintimidated by the female anatomy. Keep a rolled-up newspaper by the bed to train the *Cyberdorkus* in your likes and dislikes.

Bitter Freeloading Journalist
(*Steno conspirasus*)

Diet:

Nest Type:

Intake:

Foraging Technique:

Plumage: Old oxford-cloth shirt, half tucked-in. Comfortable shoes—running shoes or lace-ups with thick soles—for pounding the pavement. Suspicious expression. Steno pad in back pocket, tape recorder, Snickers bar, and dogeared copy of *All the President's Men* in shoulder bag.

Habitat: The Bitter Freeloading Journalist is recognizable as the one getting underfoot at the site of a grisly accident ("How far did the brains splatter, Officer?") or getting tangled with a flock of his fellows when a politician or famed defendant emerges from a municipal building. Also found in drugstores buying throat lozenges (screaming questions at press conferences), cold tablets (he doesn't get enough sleep) or sleeping pills (he *can't* sleep).

Feeding Habits: When fending for himself, the Journalist eats endless quick and easy meals of stir-fry, spaghetti with tomato sauce, and packs of ramen noodles. However, true to his name, the Bitter Freeloading Journalist is constantly seeking a meal paid for by others. If there is a sponsored luncheon, a junket, a cocktail party paid for by someone else, the BFJ is there. He is a parasitic creature, much like the brown-headed cowbird.

Sexual Display: Tucks in his shirt and wears a tie. Flaunts his press credentials, which sometimes get him into museums for free. Refers to politicians and local celebrities by their first names. Affects hardboiled, world-weary air. (He wishes journalists still wore fedoras with a press card stuck under the brim.) Brags that he is going to get a column any day now.

Agonistic Display: Easily threatened, since most of the animal kingdom loathes the press. Reacts to threats of male dominance with sycophantic behavior, bowing, scraping, and sucking up to males higher in the dominance hierarchy while internally writing screaming, scathing banner headlines about them.

Courtship Behavior: Takes you to anything he gets for free—passes to movie screenings are the most common option. Also enjoys dating activities that are both cost-effective and involve a lot of talking (the species may whine a lot, but it is verbal).

Mating Ritual: Buys plenty of condoms—he's read all the paper's health articles.

Mating Call: "You really, really liked my piece on the toxic waste dump debate?"

High-Strung Chef
(*Julius child*)

Diet: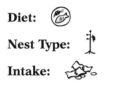

Nest Type:

Intake:

Foraging Technique:

Plumage: Toque, if he is a classicist. Baggy, comfy pants and clogs, if he is a rebel. Fingers stained from olives or raspberries, redolent of garlic. Slightly insane gleam in eye. The High-Strung Chef may not be overweight (this is a stereotype), but he usually does have a potbelly.

Habitat: Kitchen—his own or his employer's. In either case, he will not let you touch anything. Williams-Sonoma outlet, drooling over copper cookware and heavy industrial blenders. Gourmet food shop, palpating the produce with a doubting look on his face, or sniffing diffidently at the cheeses. Fish market, peering into the eyes of a brook trout.

Feeding Habits: Diet is wide-ranging, yet specific. Highly experimental, samples a vast range of cuisines and ingredients. Green Papaya Salad with

Stir-Fried Chayote Squash, Tortellini with Gorgon-zola-Walnut Cream Sauce, and Greek Roast Lamb with Artichokes. Completely disparaging when a dish is not up to his standards. A picker. A send-backer. Drives dates crazy in restaurants.

Sexual Display: Wears his chef's garb out "to run a few errands," knowing that it is an instant conversation starter. Offers unsolicited advice to attractive fellow shoppers in supermarket.

Agonistic Display: Defensive that other men may think he has chosen a "girlie" profession, the High-Strung Chef may be quick to take offense. On the other hand, he may be so secure in his gifts (and in the admiring responses of female foodies) that he feels no need to get into chest-puffing masculinity contests with other males. If someone hints that he has a heavy hand with the chervil, however, he may become violent.

Courtship Behavior: Cooking for the female. If the female offers to help, she will soon find herself being barked at as if she were a sous-chef with a severe head injury. "Don't let that brandy sauce boil over! Don't overbeat the egg whites! That's how you chop garlic?" The savvy ethologist should instead ask the Chef to take her on a date to the docks or to the ethnic neighborhood where he buys lemongrass and cod, as seeing him comfortable in an alien environment can be arousing. Unfortunately, thanks to his impossible hours, courtship may be limited to eating in the restaurant where he works, over and over and over and over.

Mating Ritual: Scrubs hands and nails in a futile attempt not to get fish smells all over you.

Mating Call: "I've brought you truffle oil."

Capable Electrician/ Telephone Installer (*Birdona wire*)

Diet:

Nest Type:

Intake:

Foraging Technique:

Plumage: Coveralls or jeans and a snazzy service jacket. Older members of the species may fit the *Saturday Night Live* handyman stereotype (potbelly plus low-slung jeans, pulled lower by utility belt to reveal the butt crack), but younger Birdona wires may possess more fashion savvy. Some possess interesting facial hair—waxed mustache, long sideburns, goatees—while others offer the clean-cut chipper looks of a 1950s cartoon of a handsome, helpful handyman.

Habitat: Look for the Electrician/Telephone Installer boy clambering up a big pole (enjoy the imagery) in a theater, on a movie set, or even in your own home, installing your new fax line. The hip Electrician boy is drawn to modern, technological art. He may be cruising the World Wide Web or helping a lighting designer friend work on a performance piece or modern dance show. Or he may be playing pinball. For reasons that are not yet fully understood, Electrician/Telephone Installer boys tend to enjoy pinball.

Feeding Habits: Because most electricians get paid for the time spent en route to gigs but not for lunch hours, they favor foods that can be eaten while driving. Of the major fast-food outlets, they often choose Wendy's because it is the most generous with ketchup. (Electricians' cars are filled with squashed cups containing leftover ketchup, stuffed with napkins, and folded closed at the top.) Onsite, they favor cold pizza, as the grease congeals and does not run down their arms and onto the wires.

Sexual Display: They wear an extrabig tool belt with unnecessary flashy-colored tools hanging off it. (Devices that are not instantly recognizable have extra sex appeal.) They wear a custom-made sheath for their splicer's knife. They act nonchalant; e.g., "Ah, the brownouts are because you've got a 15 and you need a 20, but we'll run some Romex through here and it'll take care of your problem." They talk incessantly about increasing power (i.e., "You need a larger breaker," and "This is gonna pull a lot of amps").

Agonistic Display: Unleashes a torrent of incomprehensible words and letters, designed to befuddle the interloping male: 66M1-50, M Block, Data Multiplexers. Announces that the rival's entire house is an electrical fire hazard. Acts fearless and impressive on a ladder.

Courtship Behavior: Playful. Shines a portable flashlight under his chin and makes funny faces; makes shadow-puppet bunnies on your wall; surprises you by rewiring your house; makes you earrings and bracelets out of brightly colored wire; gets you illegal cable.

Mating Ritual: Like a Wild West gunslinger, he knows exactly where tools are on his body, and when he undresses, he whips off each one off in one fluid motion. He understands masculine and feminine prongs and receptors; he knows that such connections cannot be forced; he has observed that his Leatherman fits into its sheath only one way. This translates into competent (if slightly distant and technical) sexual play.

Mating Call: "Hey. I've got a digital volt meter. Let me take a look at that for you."

Smoldering Forest Ranger
(*Yogius smoky*)

Diet:

Nest Type:

Intake:

Foraging Technique:

Plumage: All the benefits of the man in uniform plus the shimmering gloss of environmental correctness! When not in his dapper ranger outfit, the *Yogius* is usually sporting a red checkered Pendleton wool shirt, hiking boots, and polypropylene long johns. The fortunate *Yogius* spotter may espy the male in his union suit, with the little trap door for the butt and everything.

Habitat: Where the trees are. By the lake. Rock climbing. Hiking. Tending the compost heap. In his little cabin in the woods, with a pellet stove that provides clean burning, renewable energy, and runs on feed corn and reprocessed paper.

Feeding Habits: Nuts and berries. Big things with antlers.

Sexual Display: Cleans the dead leaves and dung out of the treads of his boots.

Agonistic Display: Normally unfailingly polite, the *Yogius* lashes out only when threatened by city slickers who treat our woodlands with disrespect. He gleefully (but stone-facedly) tells them of recent bear attacks in the region and enjoys chopping wood before lesser males so that they may observe his manly biceps.

Courtship Behavior: Takes you canoeing, white-water rafting, and camping, but does not grope you in the tent until you indicate readiness. Doffs cap when he sees you. Calls you ma'am until you beg for mercy.

Mating Ritual: Builds a fire with the logs you've watched him chop. Cuddles with you under an L. L. Bean blanket or the quilt his grandma made. Recites poems about trees. If courtship is occurring in the middle of winter, the sex itself is without much prelude. He has no central heating. If you linger to gaze at each others' nude bodies, you will become frosty little Popsicles.

Mating Call: "Would you like to help me build a solar water distiller?"

Wiry Housepainter
(*Cannibis latex*)

Diet:

Nest Type:

Intake:

Foraging Technique:

Plumage: Paint-splattered overalls or painter's pants. Converse low-tops. Baseball cap, painter's cap, or shaggy hair flecked with bright bits of latex paint. T-shirt reading "Cypress Hill," "Sweet 'N' High," or simply decorated with a five-pointed leaf.

Habitat: Standing behind the shrubbery, on his smoking break. Lying on the grass looking at the sky. Studying the paint, the way it swirls. Going to the van for munchies.

Feeding Habits: Frequently struck by the afore-mentioned munchies—thus always within reach of the four food groups: salt, fat, more salt, and more fat.

Sexual Display: Has his "dressy" overalls—i.e., the ones without paint or holes. Wears them with the white long-john top that smells like Downy. Offers the intriguing female "kind bud."

Agonistic Display: Rare. The *Cannibis latex* is usually too blissed out to engage in such behavior. When employer castigates him for leaving huge streaks on the garage and cans in the front yard, he merely looks stricken. "Severe bummer," or "That's so harsh!" or "Man, I totally zoned" is about as animated as he gets.

Courtship Behavior: Watches *The Simpsons* with you while you eat cold cereal. Also *Melrose Place, Beverly Hills 90210, Party of Five, Lois and Clark,* Saturday morning cartoons, Sidney Sheldon and Danielle Steel Movies of the Week, *Mad About You, Roseanne, Seinfeld, Friends,* all the *Star Trek*s, and countless hours of cartoons and MTV. When you suggest alternate activities, he is stunned: "But it's Must-See TV!"

Mating Ritual: Falls asleep before achieving denouement.

Mating Call: "You look like that chick. You know, the one on that show. You know, the show about the guy and the other guy? The chick with the hair that's, you know, like yours. The chick."

Field Notes: Do not confuse the Wiry Housepainter with the Starving Disaffected Art Male. The Wiry Housepainter has no grand ambitions, no firm belief that he is a Picasso laboring in obscurity. As long as he has his pipe, his bong, and his paintbrush, he is a fulfilled man. Whether you find this amusing, dismaying, or deeply wrong, you must admit that such serenity is rare in this world.

Bemuscled Construction Worker
(*Leerus oglus*)

Diet: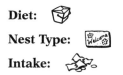

Nest Type:

Intake:

Foraging Technique:

Plumage: Jeans, big boots, heavy utility belt, hard hat, power tools—all the accoutrements that say "Me Big Heterosexual Man." (Then again, they could be saying "I am a member of the Village People.")

Habitat: Making the pavement shake outside your window (note parallel to vintage pre-disco-era song, "I Feel the Earth Move"). Clambering up the scaffolding of an office building. Sitting on a wooden plank eating lunch while offering deeply complimentary observations to the passing ladies.

Feeding Habits: Bag lunch or fast food (amuses self by dropping French fries on heads of passersby). Phallic thermos of disgusting coffee (refuses to share).

Sexual Display: Neatly pressed jeans with a belt (no visible butt crack when he goes a-courtin'). Tends to like the eye-contact-across-a-crowded-room ploy. Buys women drinks. Holds in stomach. Then again, when he is on the job with his beer belly hanging out, catcalling and hubba-hubba-ing, perhaps he thinks that is actually a fruitful sexual display. This is an area that calls for further study.

Agonistic Display: Like the tufted titmouse, who leans forward, opens his bill, spreads his wings, and lunges at the combatant encroaching on his territory, the *Leerus oglus* often reacts physically when threatened. Expect to see chest-puffing, strutting, head-shaking, and ultimately, the aggressive titmouse-like lunge.

Courtship Behavior: Brings flowers. Takes female to ball games, amusement parks, the kind of bars where the bartender snorts if you order a cosmopolitan.

Mating Ritual: Buys you crotchless, nippleless undergarments. Tells you he'd rather do you than any of your friends.

Mating Call: "Babe, I'm gonna get Susan's name lasered off my arm and get yours inked in. How do you spell it again?"

Family: Athletic

Hulking Big-Necked Football Stud	*Testaverdus slaughter*
Gangly Foxy Basketball Player	*Anfernee backboardus*
Stick-Swinging Hockeyguy	*Vanbiesbrouck lindros*
Graceful Tennis Man	*Overheadus lob*
Kamikaze Mountain Biker	*Banzai muddi*
Weekend Suburban Road Biker	*Daisi daisi*
Spiritual Surfer Dude	*Mauna loa macadamius nuttum*
Nonverbal Skater Boy	*Halfpipus dudum*

About Athletic Boys

This genus incorporates both "watchers" and "doers." For Athletic males, sports serve as a mechanism for bonding, self-measurement, group identity, and even art (in the way that the graceful flight patterns of certain Canada geese are art). The aggressive and/or encouraging call-and-response vocalizations human males make when engaged in or watching sports is the human female equivalent of actual conversation.

The Athletic male calls famous players (the alpha males of this family) by their first names, *as if he actually knows them.* In addition, he refers to the team not as "the Forty-Niners" or "the Bruins" but as "we," *as if he actually plays with them.* He enjoys wearing the jerseys, logos, and accessories of "his" team (conveniently making gift-giving easy for the female). When the team loses, his grief, like that of Gilgamesh, is so profound it is *as if he has actually died with them.*

Just as ducks have communal loafing areas where they gather to relax and exchange duck information, human males have sports bars. In addition to sharing information about food supply sites (where is the burger? where is the beer?), the group gathering serves as a defense against predators. No one will mock the Athletic male's big-necked state or inability to discuss health care reform when there are many of them in one place.

Of course, some species are not pack animals. The surfer, the mountain biker, the triathlete . . . all may prefer to pursue their sports as soloists. Unfortunately, there is no correlation between solo pursuits and increased communicative ability. These athletes still may have trouble actually conversing.

Hulking Big-Necked Football Stud
(*Testaverdus slaughter*)

Diet: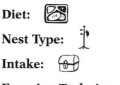

Nest Type:

Intake:

Foraging Technique:

Plumage: Enough team logos, names, numerals, and slogans adorn his oversized body to fill all the billboards in Lambeau Field. "Tribute" Superbowl Championship ring the size of a golf ball. If his time as a high school nose guard was the highlight of his life, he may also have a high school ring with a huge stone in it that leaves a dent every time he punches the wall in a fury.

Habitat: Beach or park, playing touch football while pretending he's not out for blood. Bars with pool tables. Bars with basketball machines. Bars with foosball tables. Gym. (However, the gym is not an end in and of itself, as it is for the Steroid-Addled Gym Rat—it is merely a means to an end; namely increased prowess at *football*, the sole reason for living.)

Feeding Habits: Susceptibility to advertising guarantees that if he sees Deion Sanders eating at Wendy's, you know where he'll be dining that evening.

Sexual Display: Polo Sport.

Agonistic Display: Often insecure about his conversational abilities, the *Testaverdus slaughter* may imitate the speech, tone, and inflections of the person he is with, in a manner reminiscent of the vocal mimicry of the European starling. But when he is called dumb, he behaves like the Canada goose, pumping his head up and down, then attacking the subordinate male.

Courtship Behavior: Frequent jaunts to sporting goods stores to buy weights or equipment, or simply to hang out and breathe the testosterone-scented air. Unlike other human males, enjoys shopping. The female can drop him off at a shoe store in the mall, where he will happily ogle whichever sneakers his idol endorses, and return for him several hours later. Playing ball (the female watches). Attending college and pro football games, where he chants the vocalization "They're hurtin' for a pass-rush specialist for the duration."

Mating Ritual: May make a short pass or a long pass, depending on his ability to read the defense and find his receiver. May run and scramble, as he has the ability to elude and break tackles. Still, unlike many males, he is happy to receive a pass and accelerates with ease. Good hands with either soft or hard passes. A good tight end.

Mating Call: "I think we could go all the way."

Gangly Foxy Basketball Player
(*Anfernee backboardus*)

Diet: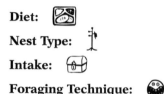

Nest Type:

Intake:

Foraging Technique:

Plumage: Long, baggy mesh shorts, tank top (one of the few species that doesn't look like a Barcalounger-planted, Fritos-scarfing slug in this item), Nike Air Max Uptempos (aka David Robinson shoes) or Air Zooms (aka Jason Kidd shoes) or Air Jordans (self-explanatory). Oversized nylon wind-breaker–puffy pants combo, sometimes worn with one pant leg pushed up to the knee (an incomprehensible trend-of-the-moment). Enjoys the opportunity to dress formally, wearing outspoken, sharply cut Italian suits in unusual colors and fabrics. Underneath it all, whatever deodorant Barkley endorses.

Habitat: On the blacktop, shooting hoops. See also community court, gym, recreation center, school yard. Watching professional and college games. In line at the ticket outlet, early, to get seats for the aforementioned games. In little cousin's driveway, playing Horse (endearing to watch). Playing imaginary one-on-one, to the imaginary roar of the imaginary crowd, against Shaq. In the grocery store, buying the breakfast cereal Hakeem eats.

Feeding Habits: Intriguingly schizophrenic mix of hearty, fatty, cholesterol-laden home cooking—ribs, fried chicken, mayonnaise-y potato salad, cole slaw, Cool Whip–filled Jell-O ring with fruit suspended in it, Rice Krispie bars, seven-layer salad, tater-tot casserole, and healthy training food like skinless grilled chicken, pasta, fruit, big plates of cooked greens like kale. Scientists hypothesize that the dichotomy is due to the fact that he is close to his mother, ergo, food means love, but desires to break free of her influence, ergo, he eats healthy food to define himself as a man . . . and as a Player.

Sexual Display: Note that the language of basketball is in itself quite sexual: baller, hoopster, stuffing, monster slam, midair pass, tomahawk jam. Merely by playing at the top of his game, the Gangly Basketball Player is putting on a sexual display.

Agonistic Display: Emulates Barkley, unleashing a withering stream of trash talk, or Rodman, getting physical. Also enjoys screaming with hostile laughter at the other team's mascot.

Courtship Behavior: In the vernacular of the species, the man has more moves than Ex-Lax. May scrounge up hard-to-get playoff tickets. May take you on romantic dinner cruise around local body of water, on family picnic, to church with his grandma, to swanky dance club or loud sporty restaurant. Has advantage of size—generally makes you feel both dizzy and protected.

Mating Ritual: Due to philosopher-coaches like Pat Riley who say things like "Luck is when preparation meets opportunity" and "Sports is the toy store of life," the *Anfernee backboardus* may give himself urgent, muttered pep talks in bed.

Mating Call: "You know what they say about big hands, big feet? It's all true."

Field Notes: Call him Money. He'll think it's hilarious.

Stick-Swinging Hockeyguy
(*Vanbiesbrouck lindros*)

Diet:

Nest Type:

Intake:

Foraging Technique:

Plumage: On the ice, the *Vanbiesbrouck lindros* wears Bauer skates, padding, gloves, a cup to protect the fragile reproductive organs. Off the ice, he may wear cowboy boots and a purple leather jacket with an elastic waistband. His form, compared to that of his fellow athletes, is near perfection: big but not lumbering, well-muscled but not thick-necked. There is a subspecies of preppy hockey boys in khaki pants—to learn to spot them, read the sections on the Socialite and the Party Animal as well as this listing.

Habitat: They are colloquially called "rink rats" for a reason. From the time they were tiny mites and Mom drove them to the rink every weekend, Hockeyguys have always been more comfortable at the rink than anywhere else on earth. Except possibly for Irish bars (if they are Irish) or pubs called the Brat 'n' Brew (if they are from the Midwest).

Also tailgates—beer is central to most evening activities—and restaurants serving huge slabs of meat.

Feeding Habits: At the rink, junk food machines rule the day. Power Bars are "pussy food." (Note: "pussy" is a key word in the vocalizations of this species: non-Bauer skates are for pussies, in-line skating is a pussy sport, fancy foreign beers are pussy drinks.) Outside the rink, the bloodthirsty Stick-Swinging Hockeyguy enjoys *poutine* (French fries with melted cheese and gravy, a specialty of hockey-centric Quebec) and Double Your Meat deals (an arrangement by which, for ninety-nine cents extra, you can increase the amount of beef product on your plate, a specialty of Wisconsin). PBR (Pabst) and Old Swill (Old Milwaukee) are the only acceptable beers in much of Hockeyguy's territory.

Sexual Display: Shows off by shooting goal after goal at a church fair hockey booth or amusement park attraction. (If he wins a cheap stuffed bunny, he gives it to the female he is trying to impress.) Coaches Mite, Squirt, or Peewee league hockey and hits on the little kids' mothers. Goes inline skating (even though it is pussy, it's a good way to stay in shape during the off season).

Agonistic Display: Extraordinarily agonistic species. The "referees" do not intervene unless much blood is spilled. In basketball, fighting leads to automatic ejection; in hockey, fighting is encouraged but regulated. For instance, it's illegal to fight with gloves on. Drawing blood is a longer penalty than just raising welts. If you're the third man in the fight you're thrown out. The flock polices itself.

Courtship Behavior: Many Hockeyguys are family oriented despite their bloodthirstiness. On Sunday they may take a female to church or to watch their nephew play Peewee hockey (where the adorability quotient plummets as you watch them scream *"Check him!!!"* at tiny boys who can barely stand up on skates). A hockeyguy may take you to his basement to shoot tennis balls into a net (if he always makes you play goalie, lose him) or to his house to watch *Slap Shot, Sudden Impact,* or (when he's feeling romantic) *The Cutting Edge.* Also skiing, snowmobiling—anything involving cold, sweat, and a high risk of injury.

Mating Ritual: When the gear comes off, they're vulnerable. They like having equipment to hide behind. Moments before foreplay are often awkward, full of stammering and pauses. However, once the proceedings are under way, hockey players are usually fairly clueful lovers. They have better fine motor control than most other athletes. They cannot win a game without the combination of teamwork and individual achievement. And like basketball players, they need a combination of grace, strength, speed, and stamina. Plus they lend you a cute, clean Rangers jersey to sleep in.

Mating Call: "Um, are you a dancer? 'Cause the Minnesota Golden Gophers need a new cheerleader-on-ice, and I just thought you looked like you'd be really good."

Field Notes: Terms to learn:

Shooting circle
Breakout
D
Offsides
Hat trick
The slot (This is not obscene. It is a shooting area
   in front of the net.)

Graceful Tennis Man
(*Overheadus lob*)

Diet:

Nest Type:

Intake:

Foraging Technique:

Plumage: Prince Longbody racket like Michael Chang's, endorsement-covered water bottle, dainty towel, Fila warmup (if he's the genteel, country-club type) or college sweatshirt, Nike shorts, Wilson balls (the official ball of the U.S. Open!), bandanna, good-luck charm around neck (superstitious species). Many choices in overdesigned footwear.

Habitat: On a court somewhere—grass, clay, hard surface, indoor, in a park, at a country club, at a resort. Since there are very few sports bars that cater to tennis players, they tend to gather in more rarified locales. They flock to friends' homes for brunch and tennis, tennis camps, tennis clinics, and weekend retreats at his law firm's senior partner's house in the ritzy suburb. This is not to say that all tennis players are upper crusty. However, it is safe to generalize that just as the California condor (*Gymnogyps californianus* Shaw) is threatened by

DDT, coyote poisons, hunting, and food scarcity, so too is the *Overheadus lob* threatened by excessive distance from an iced latte.

Feeding Habits: Strawberries and cream at Wimbledon, Champagne in the stands or exclusive boxes of the U.S. Open. The Graceful Tennis Man generally eats healthily without any effort at all, just as he manages to wear white without ever looking dirty or disheveled. This is disheartening for females with bad habits.

Sexual Display: Agassi, Sampras, Becker, Mali-Vai Washington, Luke, and Murphy Jensen: all are Graceful Tennis Men and all are absolutely ravishing. It is a scientific fact that this is the best-looking branch of the Sportifidae family. Perfect musculature, medium to tall height, fine glutes shown off to great advantage by tight tennis shorts. And when they put the extra ball in their front hip pocket before they serve, it only creates more joy and anticipation for the imaginative female.

Agonistic Display: Hard slices, stinging serves, big strikes, viciously angled overhead returns, demented tailspin lobs, cracking backhands, hissing groundstrokes . . . until the opponent is kneeling in the clay, whimpering.

Courtship Behavior: Dates at manicured country clubs, where the silver is gleaming and every blade of grass on the golf course is the same length. Teaching you, in a manner both condescending and flirtatious, how to hold a racket. If you're lucky, the Australian Open. If you're not, watching him coach the Paducah Little Racketheads tennis team.

Mating Ritual: He is compelled to give you a moment-by-moment replay of his last game, complete with self-flagellation and/or triumphant crows of glee, before he is ready to mate. He may need to replenish fluids first.

Mating Call: "Jeez, I wish Brooke Shields would just stop calling me. You're much cuter."

Kamikaze Mountain Biker
(*Banzai muddi*)

Diet: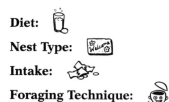

Nest Type:

Intake:

Foraging Technique:

Plumage: Hard to discern underneath all the mud. Generally includes all-purpose hiking/biking trail shoes or cleated bike shoes (depending on terrain), old ripped Patagonia shorts w/bunhuggers underneath ("to keep the important stuff out of the way"), old T-shirt or bike jersey, fingerless gloves, steed (known to mere mortals as a bike).

Habitat: Thrashin' around the local trails, giving that honking new suspension system a workout. Blowing snot rockets, cutting, grinding, and busting sweet moves until he endos and does a face plant on a rock, losing two (2) teeth.

Feeding Habits: Water. Sports beverages (so as not to bonk or biff and trash some ligaments when crankin' in the big rings or sucking wind in granny gear). Unlike the Suburban Road Biker, the Kamikaze Mountain Biker is unlikely to eat while he's shredding. He needs his hands. After a workout, though, he chows down as if destined for a Roman vomitorium.

Sexual Display: Showering. (Note: The mountain biker's propensity for filth parallels the dust-rolling behavior of the house sparrow [*Passer domesticus*], which saturates itself with dirt to maintain its plumage. The theory is that the dust absorbs excess preen oil, thereby contributing to aerodynamicism. So too with the mountain biker, who showers less than is optimal. More research is needed.)

Agonistic Display: Frequently clashes with sketchy, trail-hogging skanks with a big-air mentality. Likely to challenge them to a race, where he leaves them sullen and sucking wind at the top of a boulder.

Courtship Behavior: When not out hard-riding, the *Banzai muddi* can be a surprisingly romantic male. He takes the female on camping trips where he does the cooking over a tiny portable stove (Oodles of Noodles and instant oatmeal, but it's the thought that counts), brings her bunches of wild-flowers, enjoys introducing her to his sport. In general, he is more patient than his surfing or skateboarding counterpart, and more likely to say the words the female waits to hear: "Betty, I'd like to portage you over that rad threshold."

Mating Ritual: Showering may be considered foreplay. The Kamikaze Mountain Biker leaves a fine coating of leaves and grit on the porcelain. Afterward, you anoint his raw scrapes with Bactine and rubbing alcohol, he kisses you and talks about his upcoming ride until you fall asleep.

Mating Call: "Nice rig. Looks pretty trick."

Weekend Suburban Road Biker
(*Daisi daisi*)

Diet:

Nest Type:

Intake:

Foraging Technique:

Plumage: Like the greater prairie chicken (*Tympanuchus cupido*), who inflates his brightly colored air sac during courtship, the *Daisi daisi* favors eye-scorching colors in fabrics that pouf out when filled by the breeze. He likes lively zip-front nylon jackets, Pearl Izumi gloves, Shimano bike shoes with cleats, skin-tight shiny shorts like sausage casings, a fluorescent helmet. He has a wildly expensive aluminum bike, purchased because "it was so lightweight and aerodynamic," that he weighs down by filling its panniers with PowerBars, sweatshirts, the Sunday paper (bought to read when he stops at the diner outside town for breakfast after riding 0.8 miles), and a tool kit he doesn't know how to use.

Habitat: In his driveway, tightening those high-priced dual-suspension brakes and futzing with the clipless pedals he can't seem to get the hang of. At the aforementioned diner, "refueling" or "carbo-

loading" for the remaining 1.2 miles of his exhaustive workout. In the bike store, dreaming of titanium frames. In the health food store, stocking up on PowerBars, which he secretly eats when he isn't even biking, just to feel jocklike.

Feeding Habits: PowerBars—all the flavors, all the time. Eggs, bacon, sausage, buttered white toast—he is certain he will work it off. Often attempts to squirt water from his water bottle into his mouth while riding, frequently hitting parked cars or trees in the process.

Sexual Display: Spends the entire weekend in his expensive biking outfit, hoping someone will ask, "Are you a biker?"

Agonistic Display: When forced to the side of the path by a more aggressive member of the species bellowing "On your left!" he is more likely to shake his fist and threaten to sue than attempt to catch up.

Courtship Behavior: Endless viewings of *Breaking Away* on video. Takes organized bike tours with his paramour to such places as the Norwegian fjords or the San Juan Islands (where he often ends up panting in the "sag wagon" while his girlfriend bikes steadily along, wondering where he is).

Mating Ritual: Caresses and oils his bike until he is in a frenzy, then jumps into bed.

Mating Call: "You know, I think your seat's a little low. Want me to raise that for ya?"

Spiritual Surfer Dude
(*Mauna loa macadamius nuttum*)

Diet:

Nest Type:

Intake:

Foraging Technique:

Plumage: Rangy but well muscled. Shaggy, sun-bleached hair in need of hot-oil conditioning treatment. Black Flys silver bug-eye sunglasses, waterproof watch, baggy shorts, and reef sandals. Backpack or duffel containing sunscreen, pocket knife, papaya, Sex Wax and/or X Wax (one for waxing board, one for removing wax and tar from board). Carrying both Sex Wax and X Wax indicates an awareness of the dualities of postmodern living.

Habitat: Assaulting the hard-core surf, going off the lip, under the lip, over the lip, carving, floating, doing aerial 360s and power garges, pulling into long barrels and getting spit cleanly out. Frequently, however, he is wiping out. When the beach is all heinous two-foot blown-out slop, he may be cruising in his pickup (mildew-scented towels in the back), dented old VW bug, or VW van, pondering.

Feeding Habits: The species eats to live; it does not live to eat. The healthy surfer feeds upon fresh tropical fruit, yogurt, smoothies, brown rice. His body is his temple. The more impulsive, youthful, reckless surfer eats Devil Dogs and French fries and chews much gum.

Sexual Display: Washes off the salt. Wears closed shoes (e.g., Vans) instead of flip-flops.

Agonistic Display: The species is frequently characterized as peaceful, reverent, placid. This is incorrect; the surfer is innately territorial, much like the hummingbird (family: Trochilidae), who chases the butterfly away from his patch of nectar-bearing flowers. The *Mauna loa macadamius nuttum* often stakes a claim on a wave and defends it jealously. He may loathe all outsiders to his beach or surfing club; all newcomers to the sport; all swimmers, body surfers, and boogie-boarders.

Courtship Behavior: Early in courtship, the male may put the female in the surf on a longboard (more stable for beginners) in the hope that she will squeal, thereby arousing him.

Mating Ritual: As a precursor to mating, offers profoundly spiritual musings on destiny, the universe, nature. Not very good at listening. The act itself is brief and self-absorbed. The surfer refers to his board as both his "stick" and his "sacred tool." Indicates delusions of grandeur.

Mating Call: "Dude." (Term is gender neutral. Surfers, like parrots and gulls, use simple calls to serve many functions.)

Field Notes: Possession of boogie board as well as surfboard indicates flexibility, possible willingness to intermarry.

Nonverbal Skater Boy
(*Halfpipus dudum*)

Diet:

Nest Type:

Intake:

Foraging Technique:

Plumage: Floppy hair, floppy shirt, floppy pants, tattoo on outer calf, road burn in varying stages of scabbage. Label-conscious (in spite of elaborately casual demeanor and seeming unconcern for material goods); look for X-Large, Fuct, Airwalk, Simple, Stüssy.

Habitat: Ramps, drained swimming pools, pedestrian malls, parking lots, banisters, curbs, stadium steps, suburban sidewalk on collision course with the mincing, stooped elderly.

Feeding Habits: Portable food: pizza, Pop-Tarts (Wildberry), Slim Jims (spicy), microwave burrito. Since the Nonverbal Skater Boy tends to be under twenty-five, he frequently ends up eating whatever Mom cooks. If he lives with roommates, he may never eat a vegetable.

Sexual Display: After successfully executing kickflip or ollie, looks blankly at girl. It is up to her

to recognize that this is a sexual display. The species rarely notices women over 25; it has a universal defect in its vision that renders her utterly invisible to it. However, you can circumvent this flaw by approaching it lingering outside a 7-eleven and offering to buy it beer. This may get you arrested (and there is that statutory rape problem), but the species may glom onto you like a mother in a Harlow monkey experiment.

Agonistic Display: A skating showdown, as tense and suspenseful as the gunfight in *Shane.*

Courtship Behavior: You watch him skate while he ignores you. He lets you wear his Fuct jacket.

Mating Ritual: Anecdotal evidence has it that skate boys suck in bed. They are usually too young to understand foreplay or delayed gratification.

Mating Call: Does not possess enough verbal skill to have a mating call.

Field Notes: When separated from his board, he becomes fluttery-eyed and anxious. A girl in bed with a skater boy may roll over and discover polyurethane wheels jutting uncomfortably into her hip.

Family: Casual

Magnificent French homme	*Vraius belmondo*
Belissimo Italian Uomo	*Marcello tastianni*
Lip-smacking German Mann	*Achtung baby*
Tense but Tasty British Fellow	*Stiffupperlippus victoria*
Delicious Japanese Danshi	*Maguro nigiri*
Savory Russian Tovarich	*Illya kuryakinus*
Spicy Brazilian Homen	*Lambada lambada*
Laid-Back Jamaican Mon	*Ishotda sheriff*
Hey, It's Canadian Guy	*Overdere eh*
Tormented Bad Boy	*Davidsonus harley*
Painfully Sincere Activist Guy	*Boycottus grapesus*
Pathological Don Juan	*Sluttus virum*
Slacker Boy Toy	*Emptyus veeum*
Steroid-Addled Gym Rat	*Chromium picolinatus*
Wealthy Elderly Sugar Daddy	*Annanicolesmithus decrepitus*
Relentless Party Animal	*Hi bobum*
White Trash Fun	*Heehaw johnbobbitt*

About Casual Boys

In birdwatching terms, a "casual" is an infrequent visitor to a particular habitat. In human terms, it is a species that is fling- but not relationship-worthy, by virtue of either geography (the species' permanent home is too far away) or personality (the species is disturbed). Foreign Casuals are often met during their seasonal migrations to such places as field offices and universities in North America, Club Meds, and the Hamptons. Inappropriate Casuals are often met when a human female's defenses are down and her judgment is poor. Or she may be quite levelheadedly seeking a short-term relationship.

Note: To ornithologists, "accidentals" are even more infrequent visitors to the North American region. They are birds that are spotted only because they've strayed from their normal migratory route. In human terms, an accidental is a male you sleep with only because you are drunk.

FOREIGN BOYS

What, in particular, makes the foreign male so desirable? Let us enumerate.

1. ACCENT. Sexy. *Es verdad.* A Latin American, French, or Italian accent speaks the language of the heart; an upper-crusty British accent means the speaker must be cultured and brilliant; a working-class British accent automatically makes the speaker sly and streetwise; an Australian accent indicates a superb sense of humor; an Irish brogue means poeticism: you are dating Yeats! (Feel free to play this association game yourself.)

2. DEPTH. If the male is unable to fully express himself in English, take his silence (or the banality of his conversation) as proof that inside is a stifled, verbally dazzling soul yearning to achieve full expression. He is profound, unlike predictable American males who drone on about bands and sports and *Xena: Warrior Princess*. The foreigner may actually be as dumb as a post, but he will have returned to his homeland by the time you discern this.

3. POSITIVE ETHNIC STEREOTYPING. If he is French, he must be romantic. If he is Arab, wealthy and sultry and Valentino-esque. Latin American: fiery and hot-blooded. Russian: soulful and Dostoyevsky-ish. German: reliable (he calls when he says he'll call) and very tidy. Swiss: as efficient as a watch, and diplomatic (the payoff of years of staying neutral during world wars). If the male does not in actual life fit these stereotypes, surely you can convince yourself he does.

4. NEEDINESS. He is a stranger in a strange land. He needs you to explain cultural markers, help him decipher the train schedule, advise him about two-for-one coupons.

5. RAW DOUGH. You can mold him into the man of your dreams, choose new clothes for him, introduce him to books you love, inform him where he will be taking you on Saturday night. He will not know enough to object. Not that he would anyway, as he does not speak English well enough.

6. TRAGEDY. You both know your affair is doomed, as he must return to his country eventually. This lends an air of sorrowful inevitability to the proceedings. Females appreciate the idea of a short, sweet, white-hot love that cannot be. It's just like *Romeo and Juliet,* but without the bothersome dying.

7. TORTURE. Use him to torment local males. Imagine how insecure they will feel in comparison to a suave foreigner. Work their anxiety. Sashay down the 7-eleven aisle with the exotic species, throwing back your head and laughing at his impossibly witty remarks.

8. REINVENTING YOURSELF. He has no awareness of your history. He doesn't know about your late-'70s Barbra poodle perm or your New Wave asymmetrical bob, the fact that you voted for the mayor who was later indicted, the time you fell flat on your face in church as you got up to take Communion. No need to judge yourself or analyze your every move around him—you can just be "in the moment."

9. ROOTS. If he's from Kiev and you're of Ukrainian extraction, how perfect! It must be destiny! He can bolster your own ethnic awareness. Your borscht-making grandmother will be thrilled. If you are African-American, what better badge of your Afrocentrism than an actual Nigerian on your arm?

10. FLOUTING BOURGEOIS STANDARDS. If he's of a different race and your family and friends are horrified, excellent. It proves how open-minded you are and how prejudiced and insensitive they are. If he wears a kilt on formal occasions and your mother calls it a skirt, be secure in the knowledge of your innate superiority. If he doesn't wash as often as Americans, so what—it's sensual and earthy to revel in one's own scent. Everybody is so uptight.

11. OPPORTUNITY FOR SELF-ABSORPTION. Soul-search for hours about the morality of dating him, if he comes from a country that exploits child labor or if his nation hides war criminals. Brooding about it must make you a good person. And narcissistic romantic agony is so pleasurable.

12. FUTURE FANTASIES. Your love will last across continents, across time. One day you will dwell with him in a Loire Valley chateau, a high-tech penthouse in cosmopolitan Tokyo, a Bedouin hut in the middle of the Sinai Desert (you know he's actually a college-educated guy from Cairo, but you make do). You will have gorgeous bilingual children. But first you must have a dramatic, sobbing good-bye at the airport, just like in the movies. You will write each other every day. Your letters will be on pale blue tissuelike paper, faintly scented with your fragrance so he will think of you as he opens them. (Buy a new fragrance now in preparation for this eventuality.)

13. MEMORIES. Imagine yourself alone. He is gone. Back to the strange world whence he came. It is as if he had never been there, in your arms, in Boise. You are strolling down a path in the park, a world-weary smile fluttering on your lips. You now know so much about life and love.

INAPPROPRIATE BOYS

The "Inappropriate Casual" is inappropriate for a long-term relationship. However, he'll often do just fine for a fling.

The Inappropriate cannot form a lasting pair-bond with a woman who is his equal. He may be too callow, snide, and ineffectual (the Slacker Boy Toy); too obsessed with unhealthy hobbies (the Relentless Party Animal; the Tormented Bad Boy; the Steroid-Addled Gym Rat); too sexist and flighty (the Pathological Don Juan); too committed to things other than the relationship (the Painfully Sincere Activist Guy); too embarrassing (the White Trash Fun); or too damn old (the Wealthy Elderly Sugar Daddy). The trick here is learning to recognize when a species is just too Inappropriate even for a fling. Like when the Wealthy Elderly Sugar Daddy is drooling, incontinent, and unable to use his credit cards.

Magnificent French homme
(*Vraius belmondo*)

Diet: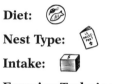

Nest Type:

Intake:

Foraging Technique:

Plumage: Attractively rumpled, stubbled, scarf-enhanced. The Vraius belmondo has a gene (absent in most American-born human males) that allows him to appear perfectly mussed—never over-groomed, never actively grubby-looking. When visiting American shores, he accentuates his Frenchness by exaggerating his guttural *R*'s, cultivating a world-weary air, and whipping out a pack of Gauloise cigarettes at every opportunity. (At home, he smokes Marlboros.)

Habitat: As he fancies himself "un hepcat," he frequents American jazz clubs and dusty old record stores. Also enjoys trips to giant fluorescent-lit supermarkets, so he can fondle loaves of Wonder Bread and shake his head sorrowfully. In the video store, rents Mickey Rourke films.

Feeding Habits: Butter and cream = good. SnackWells fat-free fudge cookies = bad. Mocks

packaged foods and the low-fat concept. Drinks heavily. Especially enjoys mocking American croissants. Will search far and wide for a decent baguette.

Sexual Display: Invades your physical space—stands too close, allowing you a whiff of musky cologne and unwashed masculinity.

Agonistic Display: Sneering. When actively threatened by a stronger male, will capitulate almost immediately, offering to collaborate, set up a puppet government, and turn over the Jews.

Courtship Behavior: Takes you to a showing of Truffaut films at the local museum. Strolling. Café-sitting. Café au lait–drinking. Ice skating. Inexplicably insisting that Gerard Depardieu is an artiste.

Mating Ritual: Puts on an Edith Piaf record, pours the red wine (it prevents heart disease, too, *c'est vrai*), sits next to you on the couch, making serious eye contact. It's all very retro.

Mating Call: Some husky, incomprehensible French babble. He might be talking about his laundry, for all you know, but he works that accent.

Field Notes: Lacking *Vraius belmondo*—spotting opportunities? Ask your local art theater to sponsor a Jerry Lewis film festival. The entire building will fill with Frenchmen.

Belissimo Italian Uomo
(*Marcello tastianni*)

Diet:

Nest Type:

Intake:

Foraging Technique:

Plumage: Loud silk button-down shirts, sometimes with short sleeves. Pointy-toed blister-inducing lizard or alligator shoes. Fur coats. Extraordinarily expensive leather jackets. Trousers with pleats and creases as sharp as Ginsu knives. Jewelry is a vital part of the look, and is not always tasteless (e.g., intriguing silver bracelets). Cologne, not always overpowering. This species has the snazziest prescription eyeglasses in the human family.

Habitat: Any crowded meeting place, the better to facilitate arguing, the national pastime. Raised in a political system that gives power to even tiny parties and necessitates the building of uncomfortable coalitions, the *Marcello tastianni* is scrupulously fair about letting everyone have a say, then shouting them down. Alcohol—Chianti, grappa, Sambuca—are fine social lubricants for this activity. Thus you are likely to spot the Belissimo Italian Uomo in bars and liquor stores. Also in candy stores buying black licorice, on architectural tours (coming as he does from the country that invented frilly buildings), and at Macy's, adding to his extensive collections of Swatches and Timberland boots.

Feeding Habits: His is a culture that truly understands coffee. Thus he downs *espresso, espresso macchiato, cappuccino, ristretto, caffe lungo,* and can give a lecture on how they all differ. Also *pastas, focaccia, gelato, granita, amaretti.* Certain Uomos of this ethologist's acquaintance treat themselves after a hard day by filling their stovetop espresso maker with grappa instead of water.

Sexual Display: Italy is the most egregiously buttocks-pinching country in Europe. (The editor of the very reference work you are holding screamed upon reading this listing and scrawled *"They're the worst!!!!!"* in the margin of the first draft, underlining it three times.) Consider yourself forewarned.

Agonistic Display: Driving. There are rules. Speeding. Honking. Changing lanes without signaling. Cutting other drivers off, laughing maniacally.

Courtship Behavior: Circuses and street fairs (it's a Fellini thing). Verdi operas. Sophia Loren movies. Drinking Campari and soda as if on Italian Riviera. Enjoys people-watching, the equivalent of sitting on the Spanish Steps in Rome. Discussing the role of pneumatic blonde porn stars in government.

Mating Ritual: Upon arrival in America, puts packet of condoms ("ribbed, for *her* pleasure") in wallet. Cooks for you. Makes love con gusto, invoking *Romeo e Giulietta,* who were *actual Italians,* as he reminds you constantly.

Mating Call: Unfortunately, the sexual display is the mating call.

Field Notes: Gift suggestion: Car horn that blares the theme from *The Godfather.*

Lip-smacking German Mann
(*Achtung baby*)

Diet:

Nest Type:

Intake:

Foraging Technique:

Plumage: Unfortunately, socks with sandals.

Habitat: When visiting American cities, the Lip-smacking German Mann feels compelled to view a beer hall, stroll through the Oktoberfest celebration, take a brewery tour, listen to the symphony's sincere attempts to play Bach and Beethoven, and attend the tiny local opera company's production of *Götterdämmerung* (in which Brunhilde is played by the eighth-grade choir teacher at Immaculata Academy).

Feeding Habits: Brats and beer, kraut (of course—this makes visiting the Midwest particularly homey for the German Mann), schnitzel, spaetzle, kaffee und kuchen. Because he is accustomed to eating Turkish food on the street in Berlin, he is comfortable with and fascinated by all manner of American street food, from soft pretzels to Nutty Buddies. However, due to his innate desire for order, he must have regular mealtimes or he becomes flustered and anxious.

Sexual Display: Dancing madly to "99 Luftballons" during New Wave Night at an American discotheque.

Agonistic Display: This vision of serene blond perfection attempts to remain stoic in the face of insult. However, note the jutting and bulging of the manly jaw when he is provoked. This is as visibly angry as he is likely to get. He may, later, spew a guttural, spit-flecked stream of German invective against the interloper, but not to his face. (Note, however, that if the Mann in question has a shaved head and wears big black boots with white laces, do not wait to see the agonistic display.)

Courtship Behavior: The German visiting American shores for more than a few days quickly learns that his odd, spiky, blond, short-on-top, long-in-the-back haircut indicates his Otherness. Thus, courtship may include a mutual trip to the hair salon for something a little more hip. Since Germans come from a country with a fine spa tradition, you might wish to introduce Herr Tasty to the hot tubs, saunas, steam rooms, massage purveyors, and facialists in your region.

Mating Ritual: Folds pants. Leaves shoes neatly aligned at foot of bed, facing due north.

Mating Call: "Vould you like to listen to some Kraftwerk?"

Tense but Tasty British Fellow
(*Stiffupperlippus victoria*)

Diet: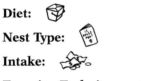

Nest Type:

Intake:

Foraging Technique:

Plumage: Hard to detect due to stubborn refusal to wear monocle, Beefeater hat, or powdered wig. May be recognized by distinct tendency toward dapperness, whether chosen style is distinguished barrister, tweedy academic, or safety-pinned punk.

Habitat: Pubs, bizarrely lamenting the fact that the beer is not served lukewarm. In line at the latest Merchant-Ivory film. Museums. Soccer matches, which turn him into a rabid, foaming animal. Enjoys sneering at the basest aspects of American pop culture, from *Beavis and Butt-Head* to talk shows (he will want to attend a taping) to big-budget Hollywood films.

Feeding Habits: The ones without adventurous tastebuds are beyond saving (just feed them their roast meats and porridges and boil those defenseless vegetables until they are limp, gray, and quivering), but many Brits recognize that the cuisines of

countries they'd colonized before the sun set on their empire are actually far superior to their own and therefore enjoy eating out. In general, the homesick Brit will seek out good, strong tea, fish and chips (served in a cone of newspaper) doused with vinegar and salt, kippers (smoked fish), and marmalade.

Sexual Display: Approaches strange woman, tells her her outfit is "absolutely ripping," "smashing," or "brilliant," secure in the knowledge that his accent alone will insure a giggly conversation instead of the buzz-off-buddy glare an American male would receive.

Agonistic Display: Stiff upper lip.

Courtship Behavior: Fusty old Shakespeare productions if he's a prig, punk shows if he's fun. Sculling. Monty Python reruns. Simply sitting at home and listening to him call the subway the tube, the elevator a lift, and a sweater a jumper is an endless source of amusement.

Mating Ritual: Closing his eyes and thinking of England. Unfortunately, the British reputation for sexual repression is well deserved. However, sometimes this extreme discomfort with all things sexual can be subverted into kinkiness. Whether this is a plus or a minus is your call.

Mating Call: "I'll be Richard III, you be Lady Anne . . ." (He lurches toward you.)

KARAOKE
magic

Delicious Japanese Danshi
(*Maguro nigiri*)

Diet: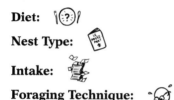

Nest Type:

Intake:

Foraging Technique:

Plumage: Plumage depends on why the Danshi is visiting the American habitat. If he's a young urban hipster, in this country to study or bum around, he probably has a cool, spiky haircut or long, flowing locks and narrow-cut trousers and shrunken suit jacket that are the height of mod. If he's a salaryman here to work in real estate, banking, or electronics, he's likely to have a serious but expensive haircut and a well-cut, sober, dark Matsuda suit, Issey Miyake shoes, Tag Heuer watch, and Mercedes sedan. Wears his shoes indoors at his host's home, as a gracious nod to American customs, even though internally the wrongness of this just kills him.

Habitat: Sharper Image store, staring at titanium camera and salivating. Baseball game. Godzilla attraction at local amusement park. Japanese bars with hostesses (the modern equivalent of geishas—such a boon during those special sexist times when a guy just wants to be a guy). Karaoke bar, crooning his heart out to "Colors of the Wind." Gambling. Playing golf. At a strip club with his fellow salarymen, smoking Davidoff cigars and leering.

Feeding Habits: Expense account. Coming from a country with twenty-dollar cups of coffee, he knows how to make it work for him. Plenty of sake, soba noodles, sushi and sashimi, Kobe beef. Soup and fish for breakfast. The idea of eating a Pop-Tart revolts him.

Sexual Display: The average young Japanese businessman has very few opportunities at home to hang out with girls. He gets a big sexual frisson from pornographic comic books (*manga*) and cartoons (*anime*). He is shocked and thrilled by American women's aggressiveness. He may express his attraction by being too forward, but he may also take things so slowly and respectfully that you have trouble discerning his interest at all.

Agonistic Display: *Tatamae* and *honne* (public and private face) are essential concepts to him. He avoids direct confrontation, as it would shame his country, his company, his hosts, his family, and himself. However, if the situation gets really ugly, a nice glamorous suicide—*seppuku*—à la Yukio Mishima is never out of the question. Now *that's* passive-aggressive.

Courtship Behavior: Buys you *bodicon* (tight dresses) by Alaia and Chanel. Makes you little origami cranes. Forces you to learn flower-arranging. If he's a young urban hipster, may buy you Hello Kitty merchandise. Rents Akira Kurosawa films, to be watched *only* on a laserdisc player, *never* with despicable, inferior videotape technology. Engages you in long, spirited debates about who would win, the raptor in *Jurassic Park* or Rodan.

Mating Ritual: As seen in *Tampopo*. Erotic games with noodles and raw eggs.

Mating Call: "Say *hai!*"

Savory Russian Tovarich
(*Illya kuryakinus*)

Diet: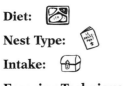

Nest Type:

Intake:

Foraging Technique:

Plumage: Cheap shoes, the clinging odor of stale cigarettes, and hair shellacked with men's hairspray are generally the order of the day. However, a growing number of *Illya kuryakini* sport sleek Italian loafers, blindingly new Levi's, and cell phones, which may indicate a successful transition to capitalism or a career as a gangster. It's hard to tell.

Habitat: Since apartments are almost impossible to get, many Russians live with their parents until they're in their thirties or forties. Being forced to share quarters with one's in-laws makes the Tovarich thrill to the sight of roomy American homes. He is overcome by the abundance of toilet paper. Since he grew up under the watchful eye of communism, he delights in unsupervised strolls through public parks and boulevards, bathed in the knowledge that there is no shadowy trench-coated man skulking behind him. Drugstores also move him deeply; he can stare at a plastic-adhesive-bandage display for hours.

Feeding Habits: Accustomed to a diet of vodka, pickles, boiled potatoes, boiled fish, boiled cabbage, gristle, borscht, and sour-cream-topped lettuce, the Tovarich will eat any and all American food. Fast food is a guilty pleasure for him, as a Happy Meal in Russia costs approximately as much as a year's tuition at Yale.

Sexual Display: Display is subtle and courtly. Spots attractive woman in bar, smiles, and raises a glass of vodka to her. (Several drinks later he may be snorting and jabbering incoherently to her while she desperately seeks an exit, but his initial pass is quite charming.)

Agonistic Display: If he is a gangster, as so many Russians are these days, he simply has the offending party rubbed out. If he is of the new breed of capitalists, he initiates a hostile takeover of the offender's company so he can assign the offender to a field office in Siberia (old habits die hard).

Courtship Behavior: Reads aloud to female romantic passages from Chekhov, Gogol, Dostoyevsky, Pushkin, Tolstoy. (Be wary if he picks up *Lolita.*) Gives her presents, like painted Ukranian eggs and nesting dolls. Swoops her into a waltz to "Lara's Theme" from *Dr. Zhivago.* Delights in Cold War nostalgia like James Bond movies and Russian constructivist Absolut ads.

Mating Ritual: Always draws the curtains. (Again, old habits die hard. Three little letters: K-G-B.)

Mating Call: Sings the *Internationale.*

Field Notes: Actual (translated) Russian jokes, potential field calls to lure the Tovarich:

How do we know Adam and Eve were Russian? Why else would they think they were in Paradise when they were homeless, naked, and had just one apple for both of them?

The pharmacist says to the customer, "In order to buy arsenic, you have to have a legal prescription. A picture of your mother-in-law just isn't enough."

How does America help heal the Russian economy?
Like an injection heals an artificial limb. (That one is a real knee-slapper!)

Spicy Brazilian Homen
(*Lambada lambada*)

Diet: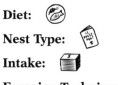

Nest Type:

Intake:

Foraging Technique:

Plumage: Cosmopolitan, as befitting a culture of extremes—from city to rain forest, from abject poverty to extraordinary wealth. Plumage may reflect anything from the party culture of the Copacabana to the influence of the Japanese community in São Paolo, the native cultures of the Amazon or the Afro-Brazilian culture of Bahia. Look for gold chains, tight pleated trousers, shoes so pointy you could spear olives with them. This species' plumage is for style, not comfort.

Habitat: Jai alai games. Soccer matches. Milton Nascimento and Gilberto Gil concerts. Browsing through world beat albums looking for MPB (aka Brazilian pop). Ballroom dancing (for some reason Brazilians are excellent ballroom dancers). Taking a *capoeira* class at the ritzy health club. On the beach, the man in the teeniest, tiniest bathing suit is Brazilian.

Feeding Habits: Look for the *Lambada lambada* in Brazilian restaurants eating *rodizio* (an all-you-can-eat festival of meat), fried balls of onions and manioc flour, or *bacalhau* (salt cod stew), drinking *caipirinhas* (drinks made with powerful sugarcane alcohol). He is a sensuous eater. Expect a mess. The Spicy Brazilian Homen eats dinner so late, most American women will be nodding off in their *feijoada* (a delicious concoction of beans, sausage, tongue, pigs' ears and tails, garlic, and chili peppers served over rice).

Sexual Display: As sexual displays go, it is not a discreet one: a male who was a stranger a moment earlier is suddenly gyrating madly with you, his knee thrust between your thighs. This would not constitute subtlety.

Agonistic Display: A macho culture. Think cockfighting. Think crazed attacks of pecking.

Courtship Behavior: Dancing and drinking. You down *caipirinhas* and *batidas* as the sun sets and the stars come out. He will never let you get the check. You will rent *Doña Flor and Her Two Husbands* and seven million incoherent Carmen Miranda movies.

Mating Ritual: Humming "The Girl from Ipanema" in your ear.

Mating Call: "Oh, my darling, Sonia Braga only wishes she was as sexy as you . . ."

Laid-Back Jamaican Mon
(*Ishotda sheriff*)

Diet:

Nest Type:

Intake:

Foraging Technique:

Plumage: Reflects his many-cultured heritage, which could include bits of British, Middle Eastern, Indian, Portuguese, South American, other Caribbean cultures all swirled into a tasty stew. May incorporate Rastawear—dreadlocks; red, green, and yellow shirts; lion symbols—as well as general relaxed island wear—loose cotton gauze shirts, leather sandals, cowrie shell jewelry.

Habitat: Outdoor reggae or dancehall show. Cricket fields. At the local exhibition of Caribbean art. In world-music stores looking for soca (soul mixed with calypso) records. At home or at a bar, watching Sunsplash on pay-per-view. In the hydroponic gardening store, buying sodium-vapor broad-spectrum heat lamps.

Feeding Habits: Red Stripe beer, Ting grapefruit soda, rum drinks, jerk chicken. Makes his own patties. Endearingly says, "It is very more-ish," when he finds something tasty.

Sexual Display: Shares his ganja.

Agonistic Display: Outsmoke the enemy. Then he is no longer your enemy; he is your friend. Everyt'ing irie.

Courtship Behavior: Tells you long, funny Anansi the Spiderman stories. Brings you Blue Mountain coffee beans. Drinks Tia Maria with you in the moonlight. Takes you out to see Ziggy Marley and the Fugees, or Shabba Ranks and Buju Banton (you may have to ignore violent imagery and homophobia). Makes you dinner with the few Jamaican foods he can find locally (jerk pork from his mother's special recipe, star apples, yams, plantains, okra, tamarind juice . . .). Sings softly to you, accompanying himself by drumming on the trash can.

Mating Ritual: Carefully extinguishes his spliff.

Mating Call: "No problem!"

Field Notes: Remove Bob Marley's "No Woman, No Cry" from his turntable. It is a bad influence.

Hey, It's Canadian Guy
(*Overdere eh*)

Diet:

Nest Type:

Intake:

Foraging Technique:

Plumage: Maple leaf on hockey jersey. Otherwise indistinguishable from average badly dressed mall-going person from the United States.

Habitat: At the zoo, homesick, looking at the moose. In his hotel room or rented apartment, homesick, watching Dudley Do-Right. In a bar, homesick, and watching Bill Clinton on television, thinking fondly of the draft-dodging pals he met in the Vietnam era when they fled northward. Gambling in Native American–owned casinos, assuaging the guilt he feels over Canada's treatment of its own native population. Playing croquet and curling. In a bookstore, picking up Margaret Atwood books and loudly announcing, "Hey dere, she's Canadian!"

Feeding Habits: Beer. Meat. Dried moose strips. Chewing tobacco.

Sexual Display: Insecure about the fact that his country's only contribution to language is the word *hoser.* Thus attempts to impress females either without language (repeatedly slashing hockey puck into net) or by an excess of language, endlessly lecturing her about the works of Great Authors (like, dere Margaret Atwood!) Who Just Happen to Be Canadian.

Agonistic Display: Mocking the fact that he says "aboot" and "oot" instead of "about" and "out," he'll spit chewing tobacco, much in the way that the eastern screech owl (*Otus asio* Linnaeus) ejects the remains of small vertebrates in the form of a hard, feathery pellet. Talk about Quebec and secession can also get his dander up, causing him to get drunk and throw hockey pucks. The suggestion that Canadians have no culture or identity infuriates him, though he cannot actually refute it. So he responds by rattling off strange lists of Famous Canadians: Pamela Anderson Lee, the guy who played Scottie on *Star Trek*, the Dionne quintuplets, Michael J. Fox, Monty Hall, Bryan Adams, and the guy who discovered insulin.

Courtship Behavior: Companionably sitting around and reading the works of Great Authors Who Just Happen to Be Canadian (Robertson Davies, William Gibson, W. P. Kinsella, Marshall McLuhan, Douglas Coupland, Carol Shields, Mordecai Richler . . .). Attending Cirque du Soleil. Going to French cultural events, where he pretends to understand actual French, which in reality bears no resemblance to Canadian French. Going hunting. Watching the Maple Leafs, Canucks, and Nordiques play ice hockey. Listening to Leonard Cohen. Going to movies starring the *SCTV* and *Kids in the Hall* alumni—Great Comedians Who Just Happen to Be Canadian!

Mating Ritual: Hunkering down beneath the down comforter, an inbred response to northern cold he cannot shake, even when visiting Southern California.

Mating Call: "So, eh, you wanna do it, eh?"

Field Notes: Actual Canadian humor:

> How many Canadians does it take to screw in a lightbulb? Twelve. Four to form a parliamentary committee to study how to solve the problem, one to complain that this joke was not in French, one to protest that the interests of Native Canadians have been overlooked, one from the National Action Committee on the Status of Women to say that women have been underrepresented in the process, one to go over the border to the Niagara Falls Factory Outlet Mall and buy a new bulb and not pay duty on it on the way back, one to actually screw it in, one to collect taxes on the whole procedure so the government can afford it, one to buy a case of Molson, and one to drop the puck.

> How do Canadians spell the name of their country with three letters? C, eh? N, eh? D, eh?

Tormented Bad Boy
(*Davidsonus harley*)

Diet:

Nest Type:

Intake:

Foraging Technique:

Plumage: Battered black leather jacket. Motorcycle. Artfully messy curls, cut short or slicked back on the sides. Wide, hurt eyes paired with sneer (think Sal Mineo *and* James Dean). Divine little denim-clad tushy. Cigarettes. Boots. Tattoos. Nicely built forearms due to ongoing braking action. Upon seeing him, you just want to burst into "The Leader of the Pack."

Habitat: Biker bars, chop shops, pool halls, vintage car and bike shows, hanging out on the corner.

Feeding Habits: Tends to eat late and erratically. Definitely not interested in exploring delicate and exotic new taste sensations—give him a burger and a beer. You're paying. Whether or not he eats depends on what drugs he is currently using (booze = nothing; coke = orders lots of food, eats nothing; speed = coffee; marijuana = everything in sight).

Sexual Display: Just as the yellow-headed blackbird flies with his prominent golden head held high, so too does the Bad Boy show off his ornately styled 'do. The thought of balding strikes terror into his heart.

Agonistic Display: Knives. Guns. Vicious beatings in the alley behind the bar (and there are *never* witnesses). Hit-and-run accidents.

Courtship Behavior: Late-night rides with your legs wrapped around his velvet rims and your hands strapped across his engines. Sitting next to the bike watching the sun set. He runs his fingers through your windblown hair. (Believes that helmet laws were designed purposely to oppress him.) You wait in the lobby of a seedy residence hotel while he disappears upstairs with a guy named Guano and comes down sniffling.

Mating Ritual: Blanket rolled up on back of bike for the express purpose of riding to a romantic locale and making love under the stars in a field. Also, his old lady might be home.

Mating Call: "I got you this TV during the looting."

Painfully Sincere Activist Guy
(*Boycottus grapesus*)

Diet:

Nest Type:

Intake:

Foraging Technique:

Plumage: Overly ripe, stretched-out, faded "Save the Whales" shirt. Clipboard. Pen. Big smile alternating with worried expression. Granola bar in jeans pocket (unwashed jeans—been meaning to pick up some environmentally friendly detergent but hasn't gotten around to it). Completely covered in pamphlets protesting the patriarchy, the gun lobby, the cuts to WIC feeding programs, racism, and militias (wakes up screaming in middle of night).

Habitat: Pondering the organic free-range chickens at the co-op. Tossing a softball in the park with his Little Brother. Going door-to-door or standing on street corner, asking, "Would you please sign this petition calling for a return to the liberal statist social programs of the 1930s?" In group, becoming actualized. At Men's Movement gathering, passing the truth stick.

Feeding Habits: Eats the aforementioned organic free-range chicken. Stir fries. Enjoys ethnic foods from divey little takeout places—Mexican, Thai, Turkish, Burmese—because they let him feel open-minded as well as cost-conscious. Constantly finding tiny packets of hoisin sauce in his car ('68 Volkswagen Beetle).

Sexual Display: Takes his oversized, parasitic dog to the park—dog attracts women who enjoy being drooled on.

Agonistic Display: Sputters, "Well, you are clearly not in touch with your personhood!" and "Let it go, man, let it go!"

Courtship Behavior: Cooks difficult-to-swallow-but-well-intentioned meals (expect many hithertofore unfamiliar grains, like millet, amaranth, and spelt), rents romantic old movies and screwball comedies, enjoys going to pet stores and cuddling the animals (may burst into tears). Brings you brightly colored flyers announcing various marches, vigils, sit-ins, occupations, walkathons, and rallies with which to feather your nest. Note that he loves humanity, but has problems with humans.

Mating Ritual: The Painfully Sincere Activist Guy puts your sexual happiness first, asking, "Do you like that?" and "What do you really want?" so often you may be tempted to get a muzzle.

Mating Call: "My inner child would like to invite yours to share our sandbox." (He might or might not be joking.)

Field Notes: When hunting this species:

Carry a copy of the *Utne Reader;* wear Birkenstocks, little glasses, and a soulful look; flash some hairy armpit; allow him to overhear you discussing your very fulfilling stint making recordings for the blind.

Pathological Don Juan
(*Sluttus virum*)

Diet:

Nest Type:

Intake:

Foraging Technique:

Plumage: Silk suit, or perfectly preserved '40s suit worn with a lavender shirt. Clean shaven and smelling faintly of Oriental aftershave, or covered with an expert sullen stubble. Beautiful hands. Exotic foreign cigarettes. Antique silver lighter. Speaks in a not-quite-identifiable foreign accent, like Kathleen Turner. Beautifully cultured, soft, slightly husky voice.

Habitat: Swanky bars with dim lighting where everyone drinks martinis and cosmopolitans. Supper clubs, swagged in red velvet, with comfortable banquettes or booths in shadowy corners, perfect for assignations. Listening to the song stylings of the New Lounge acts like Combustible Edison, snapping his fingers with a thin edge of irony, but not much.

Feeding Habits: Oysters, artichokes with butter, plump strawberries. Never rushes dinner. Pings

china and glass with fingernail to see how fine it is. Will not drink out of a plastic cup.

Sexual Display: Just as pigeons "post," nodding their heads up and down as they walk to improve their depth perception, so too does the Pathological Don Juan bob his head slightly as he scans the room, seeking his prey. When he spots it, he makes potent eye contact. He may lean over to light the cigarette of the woman at the next table or bar stool. In the most extreme cases, he may do the two-cigarette lighting trick used by Paul Henreid in *Now, Voyager.*

Agonistic Display: None. Melts away when a rival appears. There are always more women.

Courtship Behavior: Takes you dancing in strangely romantic, musty clubs with elderly people in them. The only man with whom you will ever tango. Attends revivals of The Thin Man movies. May speak in sibilant Rico Suave accent or snappy, hyperarticulated vintage Cary Grant dialect. Do not be alarmed. Know that he may cancel dates at the last minute or fail to show up. May answer the phone during sex. When you happen to overhear his telephone conversations, they often contain the phrase "now is not a good time" and "uh huh. Me too." His role model is Warren Beatty in *Shampoo.*

Mating Ritual: Prelude to mating is an entire evening of romance. Hours of foreplay. Finger sucking. Gaspingly intense eye contact. Brilliant use of tongue. Completely unselfish. Then he doesn't call (or return messages) for three weeks.

Mating Call: "I'm sorry, was I staring? It's just . . . this is embarrassing, but your beauty is truly epic. You really look like something out of a painting. There's something so sad and serene about your face."

Slacker Boy Toy
(*Emptyus veeum*)

Diet:

Nest Type:

Intake:

Foraging Technique:

Plumage: May dress like a skater or musician even if he does not know a kick flip from a power chord. Generally spotted in whatever style of garb the Beastie Boys are currently sporting. Often recognized by stupid facial hair (pointy or overlong sideburns, soul patches, goatees, stubble). Note: If boy fancies himself a skater, a writer, or a musician—and indeed, he often is cross-bred with these species—see relevant listings.

Habitat: Like many baby birds, the *Emptyus veeum* is altricial—that is, born naked, immature, helpless, unable to feed itself. The difference is that while baby birds eventually grow feathers, the Slacker Boy Toy never becomes independent. His only skill is television-watching and the acerbic deconstruction of popular culture. His habitat is the couch at his apartment, dorm, or mother's home. If you date him, his habitat will be the couch in your home.

Feeding Habits: "Ground cleaning" is the avian process of scavenging dead aquatic organisms from shorelines. The human male equivalent is hanging around until someone feeds it whatever would otherwise be thrown away. That, and ordering in pizza or Chinese while watching *Melrose*.

Sexual Display: Looks up from television.

Agonistic Display: "Tell me you're being ironic."

Courtship Behavior: Invites female over for television-watching, or shows up at her house for same. Laughs at female's jokes. Gets into heated arguments about *Schoolhouse Rock,* gold filters versus paper filters, the horror of demographic pigeonholing, Shalom versus Amber, the marketing of fake fat, breakfast cereals, and E!. Gives her gifts of pop culture detritus that convey affection without serious intent, like Pez dispensers, serial killer trading cards, vintage Brenda Walsh action figures, and William Shatner albums.

Mating Ritual: Embarrassment over scrawny body invariably causes a mad dash from fully clothed to bedspread-covered. Cunnilingus, performed underneath several pounds of Josie and the Pussycats–patterned polyester fabric, can lead to hyperventilation and profuse sweating.

Mating Call: "Wanna come over and watch *The Simpsons?*"

Steroid-Addled Gym Rat
(*Chromium picolinatus*)

Diet:

Nest Type:

Intake:

Foraging Technique:

Plumage: Quads, lats, pecs, delts, glutes, abs, traps, biceps, triceps, eyes yellow from steroid use. Mammoth arms protrude from his overdeveloped body at forty-five-degree angles, like the limbs of a small child wearing a snowsuit. If he is white, he is not actually white; he is orange-brown from tanning salons and instant tanning lotion.

Habitat: His woefully underdecorated house contains the following: tenth-grade weightlifting trophy, still lovingly buffed (much like his own torso), shrine to the Buff God Joe Weider, *Pumping Iron* videotape, Waring chrome blender for raw-egg shakes, back issues of *Ironman* and *Men's Muscle and Fitness* magazines.

Feeding Habits: Muscle-building anti-catabolic nutritional supplements with names like Ripped Fuel and Monster Max. Steroids (aka "juice"). Shark cartilage. Ginseng. Bee pollen. Bovine growth hormone chugged like chocolate milk.

Sexual Display: Squats, bench presses, deadlifts, rear delt flys, military presses, barbell curls, lat pulldowns, cable crossovers. Refers to self as "solid beef." The power of any of this to lure women is secondary to the masturbatory joy and misguided sense of control it gives him.

Agonistic Display: If a fellow builder comments on his "bitch tits"—that is, on the gynecomastia resulting from the use of certain anabolic substances—he bellows like an enraged brown thrasher (*Toxostoma rufum* Linnaeus). Thankfully, his inability to move due to his immense mass generally prevents serious injury.

Courtship Behavior: Sipping electrolyte and amino surge cocktails at the Smart Bar. Comparing body-hair removal tips. Bemoaning, as a couple, the hell that is dieting (fantasizing about Oreos instead of sex). Holding hands in the sauna, where he's sweating off water weight while you become increasingly lightheaded. Helping him rub fake-tan agents on his back (being careful to wash hands afterward or risk the dread Musclehead's Girlfriend Orange Palms). Experiencing couples' plastic surgery—you get liposuction, he gets calf implants.

Mating Ritual: Actual intercourse cannot generally occur as it drains the precious bodily fluids. He is so tanked up on swallowed and injected substances he could not perform anyway. The highly sexed female eventually must pretend all his rambling about fast-twitch and slow-twitch muscle fibers is some kind of sex talk.

Mating Call: "'Scuse me, can you oil me up?"

Wealthy Elderly Sugar Daddy
(*Annanicolesmithus decrepitus*)

Diet:

Nest Type:

Intake:

Foraging Technique:

Plumage: Light blue serge suit. White mustache (Cesar Romero lookalike). Diamond pinky ring. Hair growing out of ears. Alternative plumage: Sans-a-Belt polyester slacks, hitched up to armpits. White sneakers. The most evolved form of the species wears a hospital gown and a coating of drool.

Habitat: Swellegant penthouse apartment, sprawling tract house, or mock chateau. Decor has not changed since 1972 (or last wife). Facade may have faux columns, as on a plantation (he's going for a classy Parthenon look), or circular driveway and fountain. Inside, there may be a collection of ugly carved ivory figurines or a velvet painting of a leopard. Alternative nesting grounds: Nursing home; hospital.

Feeding Habits: Entirely too much red meat. Harvey's Bristol Cream sherry, Scotch, Manhattans.

Always eats entire contents of bread basket (survived Great Depression). Alternative: Lives on Ensure nutritional supplements, multivitamins, and digitalis.

Sexual Display: Prime sexual display is the grooming of eyebrow and nose hairs. If the species begins to prune his ear hairs, it is considered a sign that he is ready to present a young female with a diamond tennis bracelet.

Agonistic Display: Flaunting the young female is the *Annanicolesmithus decrepitus*'s primary form of agonistic display. He hopes to make other males jealous enough of his evident wealth and sexual prowess to cause them to have strokes and coronaries. A secondary form of agonistic display is the competitive recital of blood pressure and cholesterol levels.

Courtship Behavior: Takes you swing dancing (if not using a walker) and shopping, chuckling indulgently. Brings you to horse races, golf resorts, and clubby restaurants that serve steaks the size of frisbees. Takes you on drives in his Lincoln Town Car or other boatlike vehicle (pray for chauffeur). Introduces you to his grown children, who shoot daggers at you with their hateful little eyeballs.

Mating Ritual: You model lingerie while wearing high heels. You stroke his bald pate while sitting on his lap. He presents you with a little velvet box.

Mating Call: "Darling, I know we've only known one another a few weeks, but I already want to revise my will."

Relentless Party Animal
(*Hi bobum*)

Diet:

Nest Type:

Intake:

Foraging Technique:

Plumage: Former frat boy (a surefire indicator of a future huge belly and receding hairline), so he is often covered in Greek letters he cannot actually identify. Windbreaker, fleecy pullover jacket, "We're Number One" giant finger, and Styrofoam cup holder—freebies from beer and tobacco companies. Too-tight jeans (they fit last year . . .). Penny loafers or Velcroed sneakers (unlacing shoes at night is not an option when you're blotto). Flushed cheeks.

Habitat: College reunions (every year). College watering holes, bribing current students with drinks so they tolerate his endless reminiscing. College football games, screaming himself hoarse.

Feeding Habits: Party food—chips and dip, cheese puffs, Cheetos, guac, M&Ms. Ignores the cut-up carrots and celery. The most important consideration in restaurant choice is the portion be large. Potatoes must be involved. Sometimes drinks

gin and tonics, vodka tonics, Scotch. But of course, just as the worm-eating warbler (*Helmitheros vermivorus* Gmelin) subsists almost entirely on insects, the *Hi bobum*'s dietary staple is beer. *Domestic* beer. What are you, some kind of Commie?

Sexual Display: When he wants to impress a female, he fetches her drink after drink. This is his way of telling her that he will be able to provide for her, much in the way that the European gray heron demonstrates ritualized faux hunting movements to prove his mettle to the female.

Agonistic Display: Push fights lead to faux slapping leads to actual fights. In the morning, neither combatant can recall exactly how he got that shiner.

Courtship Behavior: Dancing at parties in a shuffly box step. Driving his Mustang convertible in the summer with the top down, listening to Hootie and the Blowfish and yelling "whoo." Telling his friends he's "gettin' it" while jerking his thumb toward the female.

Mating Ritual: Consider the following verbs: porking, poking, boffing, pounding, ramming the ham, drilling. Foreplay is an unheard-of concept. If he didn't penetrate immediately, he'd fall asleep; all that stroking and rubbing is hypnotic.

Mating Call: "Baby, I'd like to hold your hair back while you puke."

Field Notes: The *Hi bobum* pairs with the heavy-drinking and music-consuming behavior of the Pissy Pierced Punk with gay-bashing and racist name-calling thrown in for good measure.

White Trash Fun
(*Heehaw johnbobbitt*)

Diet:

Nest Type:

Intake:

Foraging Technique:

Plumage: "Ape drape"—hair that's shorn on top, long in the back, possibly even with a few extralong tufts if he fancies himself a young rebel. Oversized high-school ring. "10 Reasons Why Beer Is Better Than Women" T-shirt. Jeans (slim cut, as he believes low-slung, baggy jeans indicate gang membership), Coors hat.

Habitat: Monster Truck rally, pro wrestling match, Hooters restaurant, *American Gladiators* audition, racetrack (for alcohol funny car or top fuel dragster showdowns), in audience of *The Ricki Lake Show*, Jeff Foxworthy Fan Club convention, "reading" *Guns n Ammo*, *Soldier of Fortune*, or *Juggs* at the newsstand, local militia.

Feeding Habits: If it can't stand up to breading, it's not worth eating. Corn dogs. Deep-fried pies. In a weather emergency (blizzard, hurricane), if he were unable to leave the house, he would survive by unsealing and reconstituting his freeze-dried "in case of nuclear disaster" astronaut foodstuffs.

Sexual Display: Wears shirt with collar (Sears 50-50 cotton/poly blend in muted plaid, one size too small). Presses jeans (appreciates a good sharp crease). Wears his "good" sneakers.

Agonistic Display: During ritualistic "face-off," one combatant rhythmically pushes the left shoulder of his rival. The rival then replies with a short phrase like "You wanna be a tough guy?" and pushes the left shoulder of the first combatant. The short-phrase/ritual push dance continues until hats are slapped off (necessitates punching) or friends separate them with grunts of "Take it easy, bro."

Courtship Behavior: Lets you pick his Lotto numbers.

Mating Ritual: Following big evening of heavy-metal show attendance or Howard Stern book signing, gives you back rub with Udder Grease.

Mating Call: "Yer my Little Debbie snack cake."

Appendixes

*Flirting Hints from the
Ornithological World*

There are certain telltale signs of human male interest. Luckily, these are easily identifiable by anyone
who has ever studied bird behavior.

**The savvy male takes the woman out for a
nice dinner.** During courtship feeding, the male
bird presents (frequently regurgitated) food to the
female. Perhaps this is also the origin of the joke in
which the human male says, "You like seafood?"
and then opens his mouth to show the woman his
masticated meal.

A big protuberance looks really hot. The
three-wattled bellbird displays the three spiked wat-
tles beneath his beak. Human males wear bikini
briefs.

Dancing is good. Budgies mate after doing a
funky little dance of head-bobbing and beak-
touching. This is called "nudge-pumping" by ethologists, who can really sling a phrase. Cranes also
perform a swooping, flapping pas de deux. The dip-
shaking and bob-preening of western grebes resem-
ble the groovy moves of teens dancing on the beach
in Frankie Avalon films. Many slow-to-evolve or sar-
donic men enjoy this dance style. Human males
also favor the Bump.

Presents are good. The male secretary bird offers his honey a gift of sticks and animal dung. Dung is always lovely, and it goes with everything, but you might want to hold out for jewelry.

Males like to show off their competence. European gray herons ritualistically prove their hunting skills by pointing their bills downward, making gnashing jaw movements, puffing up the feathers on their heads. Human males like to open the hood of your car, stare at the engine, and ritualistically check the oil.

A guy's gotta feel pretty. Albatrosses coyly toss their heads to get attention (think Fabio).

Give a female something you made for her and her heart just melts. The bowerbirds of New Guinea build fancy nests during courtship, decorated with everything from flowers to bits of toilet paper to candy wrappers to used toothbrushes. It's pop art madness! And then the female gets to lay eggs in it. Fabulous *and* utilitarian.

Size matters. Female barn swallows measure a male's worth by the length and symmetry of his tail. Peahens check out the span of the fan on the peacock. Enough said.

Once a female has given him the least bit of encouragement, an interested male will bend over backward to impress her. Female chaffinches rapidly say "tsit-tsit" to indicate their agreeability to a male's approach. (Human equivalent: According to research by biologist Tim Perper and anthropologist David Givens, women initiate two thirds of bar pickups by using subtle cues—smiling, shifting position on the stool, making eye contact.)

Summer lovin', had me a blast. Summer is good for courtship. Many birds sing more as the day gets longer. The theory is that increased singing may increase the production of sex hormones.

It's natural to be more romantic in the beginning of a relationship. Wild whooping cranes dance more in the early stages of coupledom, perhaps when they're more insecure about the female's interest. Unfortunately, human males also stop dancing once they are comfortable in the relationship, and sit around in their undershirts watching *American Gladiators.*

The smart female has her own interests and makes the male work to get her attention. At the lek (birdie pickup area), the female sage grouses act blasé. They chatter to each other, groom themselves, preen, have a little nosh. Meanwhile, the males strut around trying to impress them. When the females are good and ready, they choose a fella and go off to mate. A lesson for us all.

Watersports are fun. Western grebes say "creet" to each other, she in high-pitched voice, he in low-pitched voice; then they stare soulfully at each other and if they're sufficiently attracted, splash water on each other. In other words, get thee to a water park.

Nothing is certain. Remember the aforementioned romantic budgies? It used to be thought that they were monogamous, but it turns out males nudge-pump with unattached females and females have been known to solicit other males. So much for till death do us part.

APPENDIX B

Domestication

◈

Almost all birds form pair-bonds. However, some birds are hopeless. To paraphrase the astute margarine commercial, *you can't fight Mother Nature.* Is there a way to tell if a given species can be domesticated? In a word, yes.

Is he monogamous? Ninety percent of bird species are. This is why Hallmark puts doves on Valentine's Day cards and elderly waiters say, "What'll it be for you two lovebirds?" However, the truism that birds mate for life is actually a falsity. Most birds are serially monogamous, meaning that they stay together for a breeding season or two or three, then move on. On the other hand, albatrosses, eagles, geese, swans, and some owls and parrots do stay together for a lifetime. So there is hope.

Is he promiscuous? Some species always meet, mate, and move on. The female winds up raising the young alone; the male is not into forming pair-bonds. In birdland as well as humanland, this is called "promiscuity." It is common among hummingbirds, grouses, and rock musicians.

Is he polygynous? Polygyny is when one male mates with two or more females. This often happens when the male holds excellent, resource-filled terri-

tory and a young female decides that being a secondary mate to such a well-off bird is better than
being the primary mate of a male with lesser territory. The secondary female, though she clearly has
let her subscription to *Ms.* lapse, gets some security,
and the lucky male gains an increased chance to
pass on his genes. If your male is wealthy and
possesses a roving eye, you have two choices. You
can accept the fact that he has mistresses (a venera-
ble tradition among married Frenchwomen, seen
recently at François Mitterrand's funeral, where his
wife and mistress mourned side-by-side) or you can
leave (seen recently in Ivana Trump).

Is polyandry an option? A polyandrous female
mates with two or more males. This occurs in less
than one percent of all bird species, but contemplating it gives me a thrill. After mating, the female lays
eggs, ends the relationship, and goes off to mate with
someone else, leaving the male to sit on the eggs and
raise the young. Observing this reversal of so-called
normal male-female roles so confused John James
Audubon that he decided the female shorebirds
actually had to be the males and vice versa. What
would he have made of Elizabeth Taylor?

Would you prefer polygamy? The male is
polygynous and the female is polyandrous. This is
very equitable and much like the open marriages of
bygone human times, like the 1970s. It's interesting
to note that a growing school of ornithological
thought holds that storybook monogamy may not
be quite as common as was once thought. Behav-
ioral ecologists now think that maybe both males
and females actually do mate outside the pair-bond,
but only take care of the babies from their own nest.
(There's also a phenomenon called egg-dumping, in

which a bird knocks other birds' eggs out of nests and replaces them with her own—essentially, she's tricking someone else into hatching and rearing her offspring. Don't try this at home.)

Will he help with child care? In most birds, parents take turns sitting on the eggs. Double-crested cormorants (*Phalacrocorax auritus* Lesson) take hourly shifts. In other species, the female does all the incubating, but the male feeds her and stands watch from a nearby tree.

Is he "opportunistic"? Among birds, "opportunistic" means adapting feeding and mating strategies to whatever the local conditions are. If there's more food or a foxier bird available somewhere else, they're gone. This is a common trait among Artsy and Inappropriate Casual males.

Is he genetically unable to settle down? Hovering is a flight characteristic of hummingbirds. They remain motionless by flying into the wind at the same speed the wind is blowing. The force of inertia holds them stationary. But their wings have to work twice as hard, generating lift on both the forward and backward strokes instead of just the forward stroke, and beating more than twenty times a second. It's absolutely exhausting. It would be easier just to settle down. But noooooo.

Are you letting "courtship feeding" get your hopes up unrealistically? It's easy to confuse food with love. In some species, the male feeds the female lavishly from the time they meet until she lays her first egg. But the feeding declines as she lays the second and third eggs, and finally he stops and makes her get her own damn dinner. Then again, in some species courtship feeding strengthens the pair-bond and reduces aggression between the male and female. So you never know.

Q & A: Why Does My Male Play Air Guitar? And Other Scientific Inquiries

Why is my male such a showoff? The male feels a compelling need to display his wealth or sportscar or penis to impress other females and intimidate other males. You cannot talk him out of it, just as you cannot tell a common tern (*Sterna hirundo*) to stop carrying a fish around the breeding colony and displaying it to females.

Why does my male think women who chug beers are really awesome? Well, the female Wilson's phalarope (*Phalaropus tricolor* Vieillot) impresses the male by stretching her neck and giving a repeated "chugging" call. Perhaps this is why he is compelled by women who can pound back the brewskies.

Why does my male spend forty-five minutes on his hair every morning? "Preening" is taking oil from the preen gland near the buttocks and spreading it over the feathers to keep them waterproof and supple. It's just like gel!

Why is my formerly dowdy male suddenly dressing up? Among many ducks, "eclipse plumage" is what happens after mating. Their shiny feathers turn dull and muted. But when they're ready to breed again, their plumage turns bright and perky. Your male's change in plumage could indicate that he's trying to win your interest again, or he could be contemplating an affair.

Why does my male sniff his food? Ducks' bills contain touch receptors that help them find insects and seeds in murky water. Your male is only making sure that his food is actually food. Do not take offense.

Why do males travel in packs? "Grouping" is a way to avoid predators. Some males watch for danger while others feed. You never know when a guy with a big knife is going to jump out at the Burger Barn! Also, the group's sheer mass may confuse the enemy. However, for some reason they do enjoy going to public bathrooms alone. Any female knows this is absurd.

Why is my male insecure about the size of his penis? Scientists did an experiment in which they lengthened or shortened the tailfeathers of long-tailed widowbirds. The males whose tails were made longer acquired the most new mates. Males with regular-sized tails got an average number of mates. Males with the smallest tails had the smallest number of mates. *Duh.* You can reassure your male about his attractiveness, but biology tells another story. No wonder the poor thing is insecure.

Why do men have iron stomachs? The gizzard is a part of a bird's stomach lined with horny ridges, like teeth, that grind the food the bird swallows. Birds often swallow sand and pebbles to keep the gizzard sharp and fresh. Grebes eat fish, which may have sharp bones, so they swallow their own feathers to cushion the bones. Your male is in good company.

Why does my male have a compulsive need to play air guitar or drums? Yellow-bellied sapsuckers drum against dried branches, gutters, stovepipes, and trash cans to proclaim their territorial boundaries and attract mates. The ruffled grouse plays air guitar by striking the air with his wings, making cool sounds and turning on the chicks. So it is with human males.

Why are males such disgusting housekeepers? Well, what are nests made of? Saliva, feathers, guano, regurgitated food, spiderwebs, cow poop, snakeskin, human hair, leaf mold, and mud. *Le voilà.*

Why is my male so territorial? Some birds defend an entire part of the woods (the *really* possessive type), others defend only their food supply (the *"Don't eat off my plate!"* type), others defend only their place to mate (the "I love my waterbed" type), others defend the nest site (the "why does your annoying friend have to come over here" type). Sandpipers defend tiny bits of space on their lek (the "you don't understand, I *always* sit there" type).

Why does my male hog the remote control? Acorn woodpeckers are inveterate hoarders. They live in environments with uneven food supplies (abundant in spring and summer, barren in winter), so they must plan ahead. They therefore find a dead, hollowed-out tree and fill it with acorns for later, packing them so tightly that no one can steal them without their being alerted. (Imagine the walnuts-in-the-closet scene from the old *Dick Van Dyke Show* and you get the idea.) The hoarding of the remote control has the same origins. The male never knows when something good might come on, as his television environment usually features periods of uneven entertainment supply. This is why he must channel surf constantly. If he were to give up the remote control, he might starve for lack of stimulus. If he were to allow the female access to the remote control, she might use it to watch *Masterpiece Theater* and *Absolutely Fabulous*.

Why is my male so paranoid? A male meadowlark will assault a stuffed bird placed in its territory, totally unable to recognize that its "rival" poses no threat. In other words, it's genetic.

Why won't my male try new restaurants? "Site fidelity" is when birds frequent certain regular locations. It's the avian equivalent of returning to a neighborhood pub or going to the same Club Med every blessed year. Familiarity with a site makes the male feel confident and assured. Can you train your male to visit a new feeding area? Certainly. Once he becomes comfortable with you, he may willingly follow you (à la Konrad Lorenz) to the restaurant of your choice. If he is resistant, though, you may still be able to bring him to a restaurant you want to visit, if you first make sure that they can make him a "kiddie plate" of safe and comfortable foodstuffs—hamburgers, chicken fingers, etc. Many high-class restaurants are familiar with the recalcitrant male and will not bat an eye when you arrange in advance for special male meals.

Male-Watching Tips

◈

Luckily for everyone, males gather wherever there is shelter, water, and food. You can even watch them in your own backyard! Look for meter readers, Federal Express deliverymen, gardeners. If you live out in the country, you can male-watch when you go out to buy cereal or go to the post office for stamps. Many of us enjoy looking for strange and exotic males when we're away from home—in parks, by the ocean, in foreign countries. Here are a few hints for anyone taking a male-watching field trip.

First of all, you're going to do a lot of walking, so wear comfortable shoes! Ankle support is vital. Break in your shoes before your first field trip; blisters are a surefire way to spoil the fun.

Get an early start—many males go jogging or dog-walking before work, or stop by the deli to get a roll and coffee. Dress in comfortable clothes. Wear layers, so you can add and subtract as the winds and temperature change. Don't wear anything you're afraid to get dirty, as you may have to step into mud or push through some brambles to get a better look at that elusive Suburban Road Biker or Heavy-Lidded Jazz Aficionado. Brightly colored fabrics and bare skin often catch the male's eye, so consider whether you wish to be seen. Do you wish to converse with passing males, or would you prefer to watch them, undisturbed, in their habitat? If your choice is the latter, walk very quietly, taking care not to step on any foam fast-food packing material or dry sticks. Avoid sudden movements; males spook easily. Be especially careful not to startle them in the woods during hunting season.

Your most important tools on a male watch are your field guide, your notebook, and your binoculars. You might want to invest in a snazzy little backpack for them, but a plastic supermarket bag will do just fine. Pack a windbreaker, plenty of water, and maybe a little snack. Be sure the field guide is accessible at all times, in case you see an unfamiliar male with an unusual pair of pants or an oddly patterned jacket. You'll want to look him up in the guide before you forget what his plumage looks like. Memories are faulty things! Take notes if you're at all perplexed by what you've seen. In the cold winter months, when the male-watching is scarce, you'll enjoy looking through your notes and remembering the fine specimens you ogled several months earlier.

You might also consider investing in a high-powered telescope with a zoom lens. Sure, it's awkward to carry, and it may result in your arrest on stalking charges, but it brings the males into sharp focus. Without mine, I would never have spotted the tiny Hermes logo on Aggro Investment Banker's tie as he was getting undressed in his penthouse apartment several long city blocks away.